Eat Smarter!

Ice Creams

30 fat-burning, health-boosting, delicious frozen treats

CARRIE BROWN

with foreword by Jonathan Bailor
Author, The Calorie Myth

ISBN-10: 149484205X
ISBN-13: 978-1494842055

DEDICATION

Geoff Nyheim

Empowerer of people, celebrator of life, lover of ice cream, and all-round outstanding human being.

Every single day I wake up and thank my lucky stars for the incredible impact you have had on my life. You have had a greater positive influence on me than anyone I have ever known. I have created a life that I love because of your support, your coaching, your encouragement, and your enthusiasm.

You inspire me to do my best work. Your integrity, and the way you are in the world is a constant, shining example to me.

You told me I could do anything I wanted to do...so I did.

CONTENTS

Acknowledgments

Foreword

ACKNOWLEDGMENTS

Jonathan Bailor – without you I would never have known what a truly healthy lifestyle looked like. What you taught me inspired me to change the course of my future completely. Your influence in my life is huge. You are one of my biggest supporters, and a brilliant partner in podcast crime. You are my hero.

The Ice Cream Taste Test Crew – Matt Ballard, Sahara Pirie, Laurie Resch, Bob Stutz, and Jen Meehan, whose thoughtful, constructive criticism helped shape many of the final versions. You ate a lot of ice cream during this endeavor, and my recipes are better because of your input. Thursday afternoons will never be the same.

Taste Testers – Geoff Nyheim, The Bailors - Jonathan, Angela, Mary Rose, and Robert - and various other awesome folks who were able to sample a few ice creams here and there, and whose feedback was also very valuable.

Marjorie Ferris aka Bea – for delivering a critical bottle of glycerin at just the right moment, and for always being willing to taste just one more flavor.

Bala Silvakumar – you make me look better than any photographer ever has!

Every last one of my lovely blog readers and podcasts listeners – you make this all worthwhile. This book is better because of you, and I am deeply honored and humbled that you choose to be a part of my world.

Mic – MVP, you're the very, very best. That's all.

Marc Levine – you know why.

FOREWORD

If someone offers you something "healthy" to eat, what emotion comes to mind? I'm guessing it's far from "delicious." And rightfully so given how "healthy" has been defined for us over the past fifty years. But isn't that sad? How could we live in a world where delicious food leads to disease-causing fat? Wouldn't a more intelligently designed and evolutionarily apt system be one where the best tasting foods are also the best for us?

There's good news, bad news, and great news. The good news is that "yes", common sense, intelligent design, and evolutionary biology all tell us that successful species are those that thrive in their environment. Hear that? We're meant to thrive, not to be deprived. The bad news is that "healthy" was redefined in a very unhealthy way a few decades ago, and that has led to the highest levels of sickness and suffering the world has ever seen. The great news is that while the world's best scientists spent the past few decades making "healthy" healthy again, a world-class pastry chef has made fat-burning and health-boosting food delicious again.

Forget about "healthy" and "moderation." Focus on smart and simple. For example, if you buy a stunning designer dress or suit at retail, moderation may be required to avoid breaking the bank. However, if you practice smart shopping, you can have your new outfit, then grab some shoes and a belt, and still stay out of trouble. When you shop smarter, you can enjoy a lot of gorgeous clothes, and avoid breaking the bank. When you eat smarter, you can enjoy a lot of delicious food, and avoid breaking your body.

Make no mistake, decades of rigorous scientific research show exactly how you can enjoy each and every flavor, texture, sensation, and exhilaration you yearn for—smarter. And there's no better example than "Eat Smarter! Ice Creams".

Moderation is a myth. If we thoughtlessly grab some chemically engineered product that happens to be edible out of the freezer of a gas station, moderation matters. But if you enjoy ice cream that provides more nutrition than most people's "healthy" low-fat lunches, you can throw moderation out the window along with your scale. You don't need either. Your body is wondrous. Your brain is amazing. Your soul needs nourishing. When you leverage your brain to give your body what it is designed to run on, it will take care of everything else for you, just like it did for every other generation of people who ever lived.

What Carrie Brown has created is amazing. She has taken whole, succulent, healing, and natural foods, mixed them with the most rigorous modern metabolic science available, and managed to end up with fantastic ice cream. Smarter ice cream. A dessert that need not even be called a dessert. A sweet, creamy, delight that is better for your taste buds and your body, than basically any "healthy" meal option found in the center aisles of your local grocery store.

When nutritious food is delicious, slim is simple. You can eat dessert first and look and feel better than you ever imagined. In "Eat Smarter! Ice Creams" Carrie Brown proves it. Eat more—smarter. Let Carrie Brown be your guide. I did. And I'm only happier and healthier because of it.

Jonathan Bailor

Author, The Calorie Myth (HarperCollins, 12.31.13)
Researcher, TheBailorGroup.com

HOW IT ALL BEGAN

Ice cream, ice cream, we all scream for ice cream!

Ice cream is one of the world's favorite sweet treats. Not mine though. Well, not in the beginning, anyway.

Growing up, my family didn't eat ice cream much. It made a rare, and brief appearance on the Sunday dessert menu every once in a great while, usually in the form of an Arctic Roll. For the uninitiated, an Arctic Roll is a wholly British thing consisting of vanilla ice cream wrapped in a thin layer of sponge cake to form a roll. It's the shape of a log, and there's a layer of raspberry sauce between the ice cream and the sponge. My mother would saw one into 4 and we'd each have a slice. I liked Arctic Roll days, although they didn't roll around very often. Ha ha! Roll. Oh never mind.

Other than Arctic Rolls, ice cream never really blew my skirt up as a kid. Looking back I think this was because the ice cream that was available back in the day was so ghastly: thin, almost icy, flavorless. I was well into adulthood when the premium ice creams hit the market, and ice cream was elevated to a whole new status. I would chow down on the odd Ben and Jerry's Cherry Garcia Ice Cream Bar, or sneak a small oblong tub of Mövenpick Café Ice Cream, and boy oh boy, did that stuff make me want to get a room. But still, ice cream was never my go-to dessert or treat.

My personal ice cream ~~fetish~~ odyssey only started some 4 years ago when my neighbor, Larry, decided to have a birthday. His lovely wife, Susan, is not the chef in the family, so I offered to cook The Birthday Dinner for Larry and his family at my home. I had the dinner down, but was somewhat stumped when it came to a suitable dessert. I knew Larry adored raspberries, and I knew the weather was going to be warm; armed only with those two pieces of information I randomly decided that I was going to make Raspberry Ice Cream, even though I had never made ice cream before. Wait. What? A pastry chef that had never made ice cream? Ever? True story. Frankly, ice cream was always a bit of a mystery to me; secretly, the thought of making it was all kinds of discombobulating.

Not being someone who lets scary things stop her from doing anything, I toddled off to Williams-

Sonoma to avail myself of an ice cream churner, and my ice cream adventures began. Being a serial overachiever, I made both Raspberry Ice Cream and Raspberry Ripple Ice Cream for Larry's birthday. Huge hits. I mean HUGE. That stuff is homemade? Are you kidding me right now??

That success, combined with the therapeutic experience I had delighted in while making said ice cream, set me off on a path that involved some 40-or-so flavors, and hundreds and hundreds of gallons of ice cream over the next 3 years. What can I say? I am an all-or-nothing kind of girl.

Never one to do things by half, I made ice cream for neighbors, ice cream for friends, ice cream for work colleagues, and ice cream for a local hotel. I rapidly became known as The Ice Cream Queen. I had strangers gate-crashing work meetings because they heard Carrie Brown's ice cream was making an appearance. Suddenly, getting volunteers for house-painting parties was a breeze. Got ice cream? I'd love to help you paint! It was awesome.

Then I learned what traditional ice cream does to our health, and my whole glorious ice-cream-making nirvana came to a screeching halt.

Unfortunately, traditional ice cream – predominantly made with cow's milk and sugar – is not so good for our health; but despite the health risks, people don't want to give it up – the proliferation of low-fat, fat-free, and dairy-free alternatives are proof of that – and who can blame them? Great ice cream is delicious! Judging by the focus on low-fat, and fat-free ice creams on sale in store freezers across America – and I am sure around the world – you'd be forgiven for thinking that the big, bad ice cream monster is fat. However, scientific research unequivocally shows that the real villain in traditional ice cream is not the fat, it's the sugar.

My education on sugar, and exactly how and why our bodies get fat – not to mention diseased – came from the brilliant Jonathan Bailor, author of The Smarter Science of Slim, and The Calorie Myth (Harper Collins, December 31, 2013). Meeting Jonathan changed my whole outlook on health and wellness, and I have now dedicated my life to developing recipes that support the findings of Jonathan's research. The man spent over 10 years of his life researching this stuff for us, the least I could do was whip up a few tasty dishes for him.

Those few tasty dishes blossomed into a fully-fledged food and lifestyle blog, with visitors from all over the world swinging by to get healthy recipes to feed themselves and their families, and to get tips and tricks on following a healthier lifestyle. In some small way I hope my recipes will help other people reach their health and body-fat goals.

Jonathan and I have now partnered up in the studio to host a wildly popular health and fitness podcast – The Smarter Science of Slim – to educate and teach people how to live a truly healthy lifestyle.

As I created more and more delicious healthy recipes, I decided it had to be possible to create ice creams that taste fantastic – and are indistinguishable from their regular milk-and-sugar-laden cousins – but without compromising our health and body-fat goals.

This book is the result.

My goal was to make ice creams that support our health and body-fat goals, and yet taste as good – or better – than premium regular ice creams. It's a lofty goal if you understand how ice cream works. It's a lofty goal if you've ever been unfortunate enough to try the dairy-free, fat-free, sugar-free, vegan, or whatever-the-heck-free versions at the store. The ice creams in this book won't taste anything like any of those. My trusty Ice Cream Taste Test Crew would agree that you cannot tell the difference between the ice creams you'll make using these recipes, and regular premium ice creams.

What I am saying here, lovely people, is that you can, in fact, have it all. You now get to eat fantastic ice cream that will help, not hinder, your health. Even if it was not a search for healthy ice creams that brought you here, why would you eat the regular stuff when you can have a super-healthy option that tastes even better?

These recipes support our health and body-fat goals by providing nutrient dense proteins, fats, fiber, water, and non-starchy carbohydrates, as well as being packed with vitamins and minerals.

All of these recipes are gluten-, grain-, soy-, and sugar-free. Many of these recipes are dairy-free, egg-free, and / or vegan – or can easily be made so with a little tweak.

Every last one of them tastes delicious.

Enjoy!

~~~~~~

"I was fortunate enough to be one of Carrie 's taste testers for her ice cream recipe development. Keep in mind that Carrie and I had never met before this encounter, and I've been making ice cream for at least a decade myself...so I thought I knew a little about ice cream.

"After only a few bites I was completely stunned at the flavors and textures of these ice creams. I thought, "How could these ice creams be so healthy? No way!"

"So I asked, the obvious question: "Which ingredients do you use?" and she answered with rapidity I cannot replicate: "Ifltoldyoul'dhavetokillyou".

"Now don't get me wrong, Carrie is sweet and generous, make no mistake about it – and when it comes to recipe development she is SERIOUS. I came away from that day with a very happy mouth and satiated belly.

"Today I am thrilled to see that she has made these recipes available to all of us."

~ Sahara Pirie

AN ICE CREAM FRAME OF MIND

When I first had this harebrained idea to write an ice cream book, the thought seemed rather huge. And a bit daunting. OK, yes. Scary. It was scary. Writing books for other people to read seems so sensible, so grown-up, so…enormous. Books are supposed to be intelligent, and meaningful, and full of information. And, magical. Books are supposed to be magical. I would get completely lost in story books when I was a young lass growing up in England. These days it's all psychology, cooking, and photography, but books are still magical to me.

Left Brain deftly tried to shoo the whole book idea away, while Right Brain was busy reasoning that I already spend a ton of my time writing stuff for other people to read on my blog anyway, so how was a book so different? Well, that's a bit logical for you, Right Brain.

So I rattled the ice creamy scheme around my noggin for a bit, and then Right Brain popped up with an entirely convincing argument that really it would be just like writing a whole slew of blog posts, printing them out, and then taping them together down one edge. Of course a book would be rather neater – not to mention – held together with something other than tape. Anyway, the thing is – as Right Brain so clearly articulated – blog posts aren't the least bit scary.

After all, this whole book thought got started after I innocently posted my recipe for Peanut Butter Ice Cream on my blog one day. In an instant I had a whole cacophony of people clamoring for more healthy ice cream. We want healthy ice cream! We want healthy ice cream!

Once Right Brain had persuaded me that this endeavor was really not so scary, I floated the idea by a few friends, and pinged a few blog and Facebook followers, to a rousing chorus of, "Me! Me! I want the first copy!" Which totally seemed like a sign. So I followed it.

And here we are, lovely readers far and wide, sitting here, on the brink of embarking on a gloriously delicious adventure together. And I couldn't be happier that Right Brain talked me into it. Because now I get to share with you a way to make your mouths happy and your bodies healthier – all at the same time – and that, is a many-splendored thing.

Once I had determined that a book was indeed going to be written, I planned on dishing up 30 fabulously healthy ice cream recipes along with beautiful images, some (hopefully) exceedingly useful information on ingredients and equipment, and calling it good; except that little voice in my head – I have a suspicion it was Right Brain – kept nagging at me that maybe there was something else that would make it more fun, more readable, more engaging. Heck, just more. I always want to give you lovely readers more.

So I did a little poll on my website's Facebook page asking how much writing you wanted in this book, or whether you just wanted me to give you the recipes already. Turns out the overwhelming majority wanted writing to go with. Who knew? If you're following along with my little blog, or listening to Jonathan and I on our podcasts, this will all make perfect sense; well, as much as anything that I do makes perfect sense. If you don't know me from a bar of soap however, some of what you read here – in amongst the recipes and decidedly sensible ice-cream-making information – may not make much sense at all, but if there's one thing you should probably know about me, it's that I do like to keep it real. And fun. If we're not having fun here, what's the point?

Left Brain just reminded me that while we're here having fun, we do have a spot of business to attend to. I am chuffed Left Brain piped up; otherwise I'd be skipping off to the Marmalade HQ kitchen to play with sugar-free Chocolate Fudge Sauce that doesn't freeze, or whipping you all up another flavor of ice cream. Some of you may well prefer I go do that. Me too!

BUT…while this book was never intended to get all geeky and scientific in the health and fat-loss department, and even though my recipes don't contain any, I do feel the need to talk for a minute or two about the big, bad ice cream monster: sugar. I want to be sure that you know what you are getting – or not getting – when you chow down on the recipes both in this book, and those over at www.carriebrown.com – on my blog.

I've noticed that when most recipes say they are sugar-free, what they really mean is they don't have ordinary refined white sugar in them. Typically, the white sugar is replaced by honey, agave, coconut sugar, maple syrup, brown sugar, or increasingly, dried fruits such as dates. What you should be aware of is that our bodies respond to all of these alternatives in essentially the same way that they respond to refined white sugar. For all intents and purposes, sugar is sugar as far as our bodies are concerned, and our bodies cannot tell the difference between refined white sugar and the others I mentioned.

When I say my recipes are sugar-free, I mean they are free of *any added sugars*, or anything that makes your body respond the same way as refined white sugar does. If your goal is fat-loss, you will do far better in reaching that goal with recipes that have neither refined white sugar nor the typically-used alternatives such as those I have mentioned above.

For those of you wondering about fruit, it is true that fruit contains sugar. This is why I only ever use the whole fruit – never juice – and I focus on using the fruits with the least sugar and highest nutritional density. The fiber in whole fruit controls the effect of dietary sugar on blood-sugar levels, and our bodies absorb the natural sugars more slowly. We are less likely to experience a spike in our blood sugar levels – such spikes being what we want to avoid. Not to mention that we need as much fiber as we can get in our diets.

Still, despite all that fiber, if fat-loss is your primary goal, you won't want to eat too much fruit-based ice cream at any one time. Luckily, my ice cream recipes are very filling, and even with my humongous appetite, I am content with one or two small scoops. When I used to eat regular ice cream I could down a whole pint without even thinking about it. Sugar will do that to you.

Talking of eating ice cream, and notwithstanding how much better for us these ice creams are than traditional ice creams, bear in mind that they should still be considered treats. A body cannot thrive on even the healthiest of ice creams alone. For optimal health and body-fat control, non-starchy vegetables and lean, nutrient dense proteins come first, followed by healthy sources of fats. These ice creams have far more protein than regular ice cream, and are packed with healthy fats. Just eat them as dessert, not the main course!

If you do want all the geeky, scientific info, and detailed research on sugars (and things that our bodies recognize as sugar), I highly recommend you read Gary Taubes' book, "Why We Get Fat and What To Do About It" and Jonathan Bailor's book, "The Calorie Myth" (Harper Collins, December 31, 2013). They will explain all you need to know. They changed my life, the pair of them.

Gosh, are you still with me, lovely readers? We're nearly at the fun bits, I promise. I bet you never imagined that ice cream needed so much explaining. But really, if we're going to do this thing, let's do it properly. You never struck me as the types that do things by half. And let me assure you, dear people, once we really get this show on the road, once this train has pulled out of the station, you'll be glad that you persevered through all this typing. Your appreciation for ice cream making will reach new heights and know no bounds! Because ice creams are the single most complex food creations we humans have come up with, and sadly, you cannot just whizz a random bunch of stuff together, churn it, sling it in the freezer and get beautiful, scoop-able, delicious ice cream the next day.

Great ice cream takes planning and preparation, especially in the ingredient and equipment departments. When the time comes to make your first ice cream recipe, you'll thank me for encouraging you to read these sections before you get started. I mean, who wants to have all these glorious recipes for healthy ice cream and then not be able to make them?? Not you.

These next sections detail what you'll need to make your adventures in healthy ice cream making easier and more successful. You could skip over all this technical stuff and dive straight into the recipe section, but understanding how ice creams work will give you the very best chance of getting a fantastic result every time. And I am as certain as I can possibly be that you definitely want fantastic results to fill your eagerly awaiting ice cream bowl with.

So before you run screaming for joy towards your kitchen to whip up your first batch of fabulously healthy ice cream, I really plead with you to take a few minutes to read the next three (short!) chapters of geeky stuff.

And just one last thing before you move right along. We need to get our brains in an ice cream frame of mind. Because great ice cream takes patience and planning.

Patience

Great ice cream is a process. The {really} good news is that these healthy ice creams are a lot less of a process than regular ice creams. Woohoo! The not-so-good news is that it is still a process. There's lots of waiting involved. Once you've made the base custard you get to wait. Then you churn the ice cream and you get to wait again. Then before you can make another batch you probably need to re-freeze the freezer bowl and you get to wait again. So you are going to need patience. There will be waiting. If you choose to forego the waiting, you will end up with a not-so-great ice cream, or a dollop of soft-serve. Then you'll be sad. I'll be sad too, because I want the ice cream made from these recipes to be the best ice cream you've ever eaten in your life. I promise you it's totally worth the wait.

Planning

Plan for AT LEAST 24 hours to go by from when you get the blender out to when you'll have a scoop of magnificent ice cream – made by your own fair hands – in your bowl. Two days is even better planning. I typically plan a week in advance, especially if I am making large quantities or a lot of different flavors at once. Yes, I know the box that the ice cream maker came in says you can have frozen treats in 20 minutes, and you can. But don't expect a fantastic scoop of ice cream in a bowl in 20 minutes. They're fibbing. I do believe in telling you how it really is, even if it's not what you really want to hear. My recipes are not recipes for soft-serve. I'll probably get to some of those at some point, but first let's make the real stuff.

Now really, I'm done jibber-jabbering.

Grab your favorite drink, and settle down in a comfy spot for a few minutes, with a cat if you have one, because cats purring nearby is all kinds of good for us humans.

Then, let the ice cream making begin!

~~~~~~

INGREDIENTS

I hate to break it to you, but ice cream is complicated. It is the most complicated food concoction we humans have created. It's all science, all the time in Ice Cream Land. There is an awful lot of chemistry involved in getting fat, sugar and water molecules to canoodle into a thick, smooth, creamy, scoop-able relationship when frozen. The good news is that unlike the components of human relationships, their behavior is extremely consistent, and predictable. Maybe that's why I love making ice cream so much. And why I live with 5 ½ cats.

Fat, sugar, and water each critically affect the outcome of ice cream, so it is not as easy as swapping out ingredients ounce for ounce from a traditional ice cream recipe. In order to end up with the right texture and consistency, the fat, water and sugar have to be in exactly the right ratios. If they are not, your ice cream may not freeze sufficiently, or it might freeze like a block of ice and not be scoop-able, or it may end up with an icy graininess and not have the smooth, creamy texture that you love. When it's right though – when you have a great recipe and follow the instructions – ice cream nirvana shall be yours.

Creating healthy, easy-to-make ice cream means replacing some key traditional ingredients – milk, sugar, and eggs – with others, while keeping the attributes that those key ingredients possess to enable a successful, delicious ice cream.

Base Ingredients

As with any other recipe, the flavor and nutritional quality of ice cream depends to a large extent on the quality of the ingredients used. If you are going to put in the effort to make your own ice cream, I thoroughly recommend using the best ingredients you can get your hands on.

In traditional ice creams, egg yolks are typically one of the main ingredients. Egg yolks are an excellent emulsifier, and impart a smooth and creamy texture to the ice cream custard. The downside to using egg yolks is that you need to master making egg custards. I love making egg custards, but egg custards can be tricky little suckers to get right, and certainly take some time. I wanted to make your ice-cream-making experience as easy and fast as possible, so while eggs are a great addition to a healthy lifestyle, I chose to develop these ice creams without the use of egg yolks, to avoid you having to master making egg custards, and so you get perfect ice cream quicker. I am pretty sure you love the idea of perfect ice cream, quicker. Ice cream that doesn't take 3 months in culinary school to prepare for.

I list here the specific base ingredients that I use for my egg-yolk-less custards, so that you can recreate these ice creams to taste exactly as they were in the Marmalade HQ kitchen. Ice creams generally have very light, subtle flavors, so changes in the base ingredients are more noticeable. Of course you are free to use different brands, but the finished ice creams will taste slightly different – or a lot different – depending on the brand you use. This is not necessarily a bad thing, I just thought it best to point it out so your expectations are set. I do like to be clear and thorough. Especially when it comes to recipes, choosing paint colors, building kitchen cabinets, and scheduling my next exhilarating road trip adventure.

Coconut Milk

Thick – this is full-fat, very thick, comes in a can, and solidifies in the 'fridge. It is made from coconut meat, and is very high in very healthy fats, especially MCTs (Medium Chain Triglycerides). I won't bore you with the technical details of MCTs – just know that they are extremely good for you. Thick coconut milk helps create a smooth and creamy texture.

Make sure that you buy it unsweetened, and shake the can very well before you open it. You can find it in most grocery stores and is often located with the Asian and / or Indian foods. I used Thai Kitchen Unsweetened Coconut Milk for the recipes in this book.

Thin – this comes in a carton and is thin like cow's milk, but is very white. It does not become thick when cold. Make sure that you buy it unsweetened. I used Trader Joe's Unsweetened Coconut Milk Beverage for the recipes in this book.

Be sure to use 'thick' or 'thin' coconut milks as noted in the recipe. They are not interchangeable, and it will make a big difference if you don't use the one called for.

Other Non-Dairy Milks

Hemp – this comes in a carton and is thin like cow's milk, but has a slight caramel color to it. Yes, it is made from hemp seeds which come from the cannabis plant; no, you will not get high off of it. Well, if you make fabulous ice cream with it you might, but it won't be the same kind of high.

Make sure that you buy it unsweetened. I used Living Harvest Unsweetened Original Hemp Milk for the recipes in this book.

Almond – this comes in a carton and is thin like cow's milk, but is darker in color. It is made from soaked almonds, so nut allergy sufferers beware. You can make your own almond milk at home, but honestly, who has time for that? Or the money, come to think of it. I'd rather be making ice cream. Or pottering in the garden. I do love a good potter.

Make sure that you buy it unsweetened. I used Trader Joe's Unsweetened Vanilla Almond Milk for the recipes in this book.

Xylitol

Xylitol is the natural sweetener that I use instead of sugar, because sugar makes you fatter faster than anything, and I'll hazard a guess that you don't want ice cream that makes you fatter. Xylitol has the same bulk and sweetness as sugar, but is a sugar alcohol which is not digested in the same way as other sugars are. Xylitol is safe for diabetics as it has a negligible glycemic load. A few people may experience slight intestinal discomfort when they start eating xylitol, but with regular consumption this goes away – don't ask me how I know.

The brand I use for the recipes in this book is Xyla, because it is made with 100% hardwoods (typically birch bark), and not corn. I do not recommend xylitol that is made with corn.

Xylitol is readily available online, but is increasingly available in grocery stores. I buy it online and in bulk because I get through so much of it in recipe development that it is a lot cheaper per pound that way. You could start a xylitol co-op!

In the sugar-free marshmallow recipe I specify powdered xylitol. I urge you to buy this ready powdered, and not attempt to make your own. I thought it would be as easy as slinging some regular xylitol in the Vitamix and switching it on. No siree. Those lovely xylitol producers have something far more powerful than even a Vitamix for pulverizing stuff to a dust. Powdered xylitol is imperceptible on the tongue and dissolves in a heartbeat – you will not get that result from your home blender. Sad, but true.

Dog owners please note: like chocolate, xylitol is dangerous to dogs – do not let them share your xylitol-containing goodies!

Vanilla 100% Whey Protein Powder

Whey protein is one of the best sources of protein, and is extremely useful in increasing our protein intake. I use 100% whey protein powder in some of my ice cream bases to dramatically increase the protein content, and make them more satiating.

Be aware that not all whey protein powders are the same – AT ALL. Most whey protein powders are high in sugar and have low quality protein. Make sure you use a 100% whey protein powder that has minimal sugars, high quality protein, and one that is instantized. This means that it mixes very easily into liquids. This is important because I'll bet you don't want lumpy ice cream. You also don't want to have to blend the heck out of your ice cream base to get the lumps out. Here's why: over-blending will materially affect the final texture and consistency of your ice cream. More on that in the mixing section. Stay tuned.

I use the same flavor – vanilla – for every recipe. I did this because I care about your budget and this lowers the number of ingredients you have to keep on hand in your pantry. I use Optimum Nutrition Gold Standard 100% Whey Vanilla Protein Powder which I buy online in 10lb bags to reduce the per pound cost to a minimum. I particularly recommend that you use the same 100% whey as I do - if possible - as different whey powders all taste different. Please note that I am not compensated by Optimum Nutrition in any way. Darn it.

Powdered Egg Whites

Egg whites are one of the best sources of protein, and are extremely useful in increasing our protein intake. I use powdered egg whites in some of my ice cream bases to dramatically increase the protein content, and make them more satiating. Déjà vu.

Using powdered egg whites instead of whey protein powder to increase the protein content is particularly useful for people who need or want a dairy-free ice cream option.

Where the recipe specifies powdered egg whites, do not substitute with fresh egg whites as you will alter the ratio of water in the ice cream custard. This will not end well.

You cannot switch out powdered egg whites for 100% whey protein powder or vice versa in these recipes. Well, you can, but you will not like the result. Believe me, I tried on your behalf, because I know what you're like.

I used Honeyville Farms Powdered Egg Whites for the recipes in this book.

Heavy (double) Cream

I use small amounts of heavy (double) cream in many of my ice cream bases because it imparts a particularly smooth and creamy result, as well as an extra depth of flavor. I do love me the odd dollop of cream.

Look for heavy (double) cream that does not say UHT on the carton. UHT cream has been treated at very high temperatures to give it a long shelf-life, but that heating also destroys the flavor. I never really understood why cream would need a long shelf-life. If it gets as far as my 'fridge, it won't be there on the shelf for long.

I recommend that you use cream that has no added ingredients, and if you can find organic cream, with no hormones or antibiotics, and from grass-fed cows, so much the better.

If you need to make a recipe dairy-free, replace the heavy (double) cream with thick coconut milk. The taste and texture will not be the same, but it will be close.

Guar gum

Since my ice creams do not use egg yolks to emulsify them, I use guar gum to help give a very smooth and creamy emulsion, and to improve the texture of the finished, frozen ice cream. Guar gum is made from ground guar beans and is an emulsifier and thickener. It also does magical things to ice crystals. We love that.

Do not be tempted to switch out guar gum with xanthan gum – they are not interchangeable when it comes to ice cream. I knew you'd want to ask me, so I thought I'd just put it straight out there.

When making your ice cream base, be careful to follow the instructions and add the guar gum last, and do not blend the ice cream base for longer than 10 seconds after you have added it. If you over mix the base after the guar gum is added you will get a very gluey, chewy ice cream.

Guar gum is readily available online and increasingly available in grocery stores. Guar gum is not cheap, but you only use tiny amounts, so it will last you a long, long time. Store guar gum in an air-tight jar. I used Bob's Red Mill brand guar gum in these recipes.

Sea salt

Salt is used to brighten the delicate flavors in ice cream and to stop them from tasting flat. I highly recommend using coarse sea salt instead of regular table salt, both for the improved flavor, and the higher concentration of minerals found in sea salt. Oh, and measure it. It takes 1 second longer. Salt is not a good ice cream flavor if your eye-balling goes a bit awry.

Additional Ingredients

Alcohol

Alcohol has two uses in ice cream – it adds flavor and inhibits freezing. A splash of liquor can transform the flavor of an ice cream from ordinary to fantastic, and most usually with just a very small amount. It can also be used in small amounts to alter the texture and consistency of the finished frozen ice cream. Altering the freeze-ability of ice cream does not require much alcohol, while adding a lot will prevent your ice cream from freezing at all. This is why people typically do not feel cold when they've been on the jolly juice. They either can't feel it, or they don't care.

I buy miniature bottles both to minimize the cost and so I don't have loads of spirits lying around the joint looking for trouble. I don't want the cats getting into it.

Butter

There's not a lot of butter involved in these recipes, but when there is some called for, I highly recommend using butter from grass-fed cows, produced without the use of hormones or antibiotics. I use Kerrygold Irish Butter in my recipes. It's awesome and it reminds me of my homeland. I'm British, it's close enough.

<u>Cocoa Powder, 100% Chocolate, and Cocoa Nibs</u>

My preferred brand for all things chocolate is Valrhona, which is made in France. It's kinda pricey and is not always readily available everywhere…but the flavor and the smoothness? Oooh la la! If you can get it, I thoroughly recommend using it.

Valrhona's Head Chocolatier is Frederic Bau, and he can do things with chocolate that would make you gasp out loud and your knees wobble. Frederic kissed me once. I didn't wash for a week. I should clarify that this incident has nothing to do with my belief that Valrhona is the best chocolate on earth. The French kiss everything.

If you can't find Valrhona, buy the best cocoa products that you have available. Other good brands in the US are Ghirardelli and Scharffenberger.

Cocoa powder / cacao / raw cocoa must be unsweetened – always read the label to verify. There should be nothing but cocoa in it. Some manufacturers can be pretty darn sneaky these days. One of my life mottos is "Read the label!" Words to live by, right there.

100% chocolate (which has no sugar in it) can be harder to find, but Ghirardelli and Scharffenberger both make it in retail packs. Any chocolate which has a lower percentage of cocoa in it than 100%, has sugar in it – and the lower the % of cocoa, the higher the % of sugar. Most people cannot eat 100% chocolate on its own as it is very bitter; it needs recipes developed specifically for it to be edible. The very good news is that your 100% chocolate stash won't go missing from the pantry when you're not looking. Well, it might once, but never a second time.

Cocoa nibs are whole cocoa beans that have been roasted and then crushed into little pieces. They are 100% cocoa. They are slightly bitter-tasting, but can add a deep chocolate flavor and great crunch when used well in recipes. I use them instead of chocolate chips, since chocolate chips have sugar in them and we don't want any of that sugar shenanigans going on.

I used Valrhona 100% Cocoa Powder, Ghirardelli 100% Cacao Unsweetened Chocolate, and Valrhona Cocoa Nibs in these recipes.

<u>Extracts / essences</u>

Extracts and essences are concentrated natural flavors – the base used is typically either alcohol or oil – that allow the addition of a whole lot of flavor without adding a whole ton of stuff. Think adding half a teaspoon of orange extract instead of 2 whole oranges. Extracts and essences can intensify the flavor of the ice cream without changing the ratio of fat, water and sugar in the custard.

Always use pure extracts and essences with no added sugar, and be sure that you are buying extracts or essences, and not flavorings. Avoid anything that has "imitation" or "artificial" on the label. We only want the real deal in our ice creams. Oh, and in our bodies.

Fruits

These recipes focus on using only the most nutrient dense fruits, and those with the lowest amounts of sugar – mainly berries and citrus. Choose the best quality and freshest fruits available. For the most nutrition, use fruits when they are naturally in season, although frozen berries are very useful as they are typically cheaper than fresh, and can mean affordable fabulous fruit ice creams in the middle of winter. When buying frozen berries make sure they are unsweetened. I like to buy fresh berries in bulk (or pay a visit to a local pick-your-own farm) when they are in season, and freeze them so I have a supply all year.

Glycerin

Glycerin is extremely useful in small amounts to stop things from freezing too hard, and also to improve texture. Like xylitol, glycerin is a sugar alcohol that has a negligible glycemic load, being digested differently to regular sugars. Glycerin is 60% as sweet as regular sugar, and derived from fats, typically coconut if it is vegetable glycerin. Glycerin performs wizardry in recipes where it is included. Yes, I know you are a little wary of strange ingredients you haven't used before, but you cannot swap out or leave out the glycerin from a recipe and still get a successful result. The recipes that use it rely on it to do their thing. Get yourself some glycerin. It also makes a fantastic skin moisturizer. Would I lie to you about baby soft skin?

I use vegetable glycerin in my recipes – make sure it is food grade – which is readily available online if you cannot find it in local stores. In stores it's best to just ask because sometimes it is with the skin care, sometimes it is with the supplements, sometimes with the first aid, and sometimes in the pharmacy. This stuff gets around a bit.

Konjac Flour (Glucomannan Powder)

I use konjac flour – also known as glucomannan powder – to replace cornstarch or flour as a thickener. It is a soluble plant fiber that thickens with 10x the power of cornstarch, so a little goes a very long way. It is tasteless, easy to use, and can be used in all sorts of cooking applications for thickening and gelling. It is readily available online or in stores that sell supplements.

Nuts

Nuts are a great way to add crunch and flavor to ice creams. Always use fresh nuts as they contain oils which will go rancid over time, and especially in warm conditions. It is best to store nuts in the freezer to keep them as fresh as possible.

Many recipes call for the nuts to be toasted. The easiest way to do this is to spread them on a cookie sheet and pop them under the broiler (grill), turning them regularly. Nuts can burn very quickly, so don't walk away once the nuts are under the heat. No one likes burnt nuts.

When buying coconut, always make sure it is unsweetened; check the label to be sure – there is a lot of sneaky sugar-adding going on in many brands. You need to be your very own Food Police.

17

Spices

Spices are awesome. They can perk up the most ordinary of dishes into something rather swoon-worthy. Cardamom is my favorite spice ever. I first ate it in San Francisco, and I have loved that city ever since.

I prefer to buy my spices in small amounts, as I need them, from a store that sells them loose, rather than buying pre-packaged jars that I may not use up before they go stale and lose their potency. Spices sold in jars are also significantly more expensive than buying loose. Store spices in air-tight glass containers, and keep them in a cool, dark place.

EQUIPMENT

In the equipment department, the only thing you MUST have is a churner, so don't panic thinking that you're going to have to mortgage the house to make these healthy ice creams – you're not. Everything else listed here just makes it easier, and quicker, but since I know you'll ask me what stuff I use, I thought I'd just give you the list upfront.

Ice Cream Churner

There's lots to choose from, ranging from super-duper, super-expensive commercial models, to buckets with rock salt round them. I am only going to tell you which ones I have because these puppies are brilliant (I have two churners and 4 freezer bowls), and between them they have churned hundreds and hundreds of gallons of ice cream perfectly. And I don't mean any old ice cream – I mean "that was the best ice cream I've eaten in my life" ice cream. So don't think for one second that you have to go all big and fancy here – you don't. This one is all you need. It's a Cuisinart ICE-20 Automatic 1 ½ Quart Ice Cream Maker. If you want to look at other brands I recommend that you read as many consumer reviews as you can before making your decision.

Weighing Scale

If you follow my blog I can just imagine your eyes rolling right around your sockets about now, because you've heard me beat this drum SO. MANY. TIMES. Oh, and here she goes again.

There is only one way to get accurate, consistent, fantastic results every single time you make great ice cream, and that is to weigh your non-liquid ingredients. Cups are handy, and super useful for liquids, but they are just not accurate enough for consistent results when ratios of ingredients matter. I weigh everything. Every time.

The scale I use has a flat weighing plate, a pull-out digital display, and weighs in both metric and imperial. It also has the ability to zero out what is on the display so you can weigh directly into the container, bowl or blender jug of your choice, which means less work and less dirty dishes.

We love that.

If you don't have a kitchen scale, please avail yourself of one. Trade in your bathroom scale for one, put one on your Christmas list, bat your eyes at your spouse, or barter your homegrown lettuces in exchange for one. Just get one. Please. Thank you.

<u>High Powered Blender OR Blender OR Food processor</u>

A Vitamix or Blendtec will be your very best friend for ice cream. Smooth, smooth, smooth. These machines smash everything that goes in them into liquid – except raspberry seeds – and believe me, I have tried to pulverize those suckers on numerous occasions. Notwithstanding the raspberry seed issue, high powered blenders are amazing. I even take mine on vacation with me, and I would not joke about such things.

I also have a second jug for my Vitamix – I find having a second blending container incredibly handy. Or maybe I just don't like washing up when I am on a roll in the kitchen. Either way, second blending jug = goodness.

I have a Kitchen Aid 5-speed blender in addition to my Vitamix for those times when I don't want to pulverize everything into oblivion. Some things don't require the extra power. I use my regular blender when I don't want or need to use the Vitamix. Grinding nuts is a great example – try grinding nuts in a Vitamix and you'll have awesome nut butter, but you won't have any ground nuts.

I also have a Cuisinart Elite 14-cup Food Processor. It comes with three bowls that sit inside one another so you can do three different things before you have to wash up, and I love that. It also has a large capacity, which I find very useful when making large batches of ice cream. Or anything else, come to think of it. I find some ice cream recipes easier to get out of a food processor than a Vitamix. Your call.

If you have one of the three you'll be good for making great ice cream.

<u>Melamine Pouring Bowls</u>

The next most important things after my churners, scale, and blender are my melamine pouring batter bowls. Melamine means they do not transfer flavors and colors like plastic, but they are way lighter than glass. They have handles and spouts, and they are the perfect solution for ice cream because you use them to store the ice cream custard in while it's in the 'fridge, and then you can pour it straight from there into the ice cream churner when it's chilled. This saves time, and more importantly, a lot of wasted ice cream custard because you are not transferring from one container to another. Plus, they make pouring your custard into your churner super-easy and super-clean; which means less clean up. I know you want less clean up.

I have lots of these bowls. They even stack neatly when not in use. I make them stackable in the 'fridge by putting a dinner plate on the top of them. When you make as much ice cream as I do, making them stackable in the 'fridge is essential. If I am doing a huge quantity or a number of different flavors of ice cream all at the same time, and my 'fridge cannot accommodate enough of these batter bowls, I use lidded Pyrex glass storage dishes (see below) to store the ice cream custards in the 'fridge. They are a lot more compact than batter bowls and readily stackable. Either work well. Pouring batter bowls are my first choice.

Spatulas

You can never have too many flexible spatulas lying around when you're in the middle of ice cream production. You specifically need spatulas that will not damage the inside of your ice cream machine's freezer bowl while you're removing the ice cream. Rubber is good, as is silicone. Smooth and super flexible is the kind of spatulas we are after.

I use the plastic spatulas that came with my ice cream churners ONLY for removing ice cream from the machine, because they are perfect for this task and I want to keep them in tip-top condition.

Sieves

I am a perfectionist, so I use sieves a lot. A lot. Strawberry seeds in the sauce? Sieve. Hazelnut skins? Sieve. Cocoa powder? Sieve. Nut dust in the nuts you just chopped? Sieve. Ice cream custards? Sieve. I sieve everything in the name of texture perfection. And when it comes to ice cream – in my little world – texture perfection is mandatory. Sieving is important.

I'll forgive you for not having sieve-itis with most things, but not when it comes to ice cream. You need a sieve (or two). And you need those sieves to be really good fine mesh sieves. These are not your regular flour-sifting sieves. When I say fine, I mean *really* fine. The kind of fine that will stop strawberry seeds in their tracks. With traditional egg-based ice creams I sieve every single custard. You won't need to do that with all of my ice cream recipes, but some of them you will, so where it says in the recipe instructions to sieve, please do. I have 3 fine mesh sieves in different sizes. Please buy at least one really good fine mesh sieve. Thank you.

Pyrex Glass Storage

I am not a fan of plastic for storage. At all. I use glass Pyrex lidded dishes for storing my ice cream in the freezer. If plastic is capable of absorbing colors and flavors, it follows that the plastic is not impermeable. The thought that the chemicals in plastic are merrily transferring back into my ice cream is highly unpleasant to me. In the Brown house, it's got to be glass. Specifically, I use the Pyrex 7-cup round dishes for ice cream storage.

Other Equipment

I also have on hand:

- Glass mixing bowls
- Electric hand mixer
- Knives
- Measuring cups (for liquids)
- Measuring spoons (for spices, extracts, guar gum, etc)
- Microplanes (for zesting)
- Whisks – small, medium, large

MIXING, CHURNING, AND FREEZING

Mixing, churning and freezing play critical roles in the production of great ice cream. How you mix, churn and freeze your ice cream custard can make a significant difference to the final result. The difference between ice cream and gelato, for example, is nothing to do with ingredients or ratios, and everything to do with how it is churned. Mixing, churning, and freezing are really important, so I implore you to pay attention. And I don't implore very often.

Before we start mixing and churning the ice cream custard, you should be aware that the flavors only fully develop once they are completely frozen. The finished frozen ice cream will taste different from both the liquid custard, and from the freshly churned ice cream in your churner, so bear that in mind when you're licking that spatula! I recommend keeping your spoons on hold until the ice cream is completely frozen in the freezer. You cannot judge an ice cream by its custard.

Ice cream making is actually pretty complicated, scientifically speaking. There's a whole bunch of geekery around getting ice crystals to form the right way, not getting them to freeze too hard, or too soft, and other thrilling physics dilemmas to think about - and there are tons of little tips and tricks that will help you get that perfect scoop of deliciousness every time.

Even if you are not new to the world of homemade ice cream, you are new to these healthy ice creams, and these custards do not behave like traditional ice cream custards. Yes, I am about to implore, again. After waiting this long for fabulously healthy ice cream recipes – and getting this far in the book – I don't want you to be disappointed with your results.

I highly recommend making a few of the simpler recipes first so you get a feel for how these ice cream custards behave, and so you know what to expect. Then, when you make the more complex ones you'll be a Pro.

Mixing

We need to get serious for a minute, and talk about air. Because air is really important in Ice Cream Land. The incorporation of air into ice cream custards during mixing will materially change the outcome of your final frozen ice cream, and it all depends on how you mix and for how long you mix.

Traditional ice creams made with an egg custard have very little air incorporated into them in the mixing stage. This produces that dense, creamy texture that we all love about premium ice cream. Cheaper ice creams have a lot of air pumped into them during mixing, which produces a much lighter, fluffier ice cream. Light and fluffy is great for the manufacturers since they are essentially selling a lot of air and a little bit of ice cream. This is one of the reasons that premium ice creams are more expensive – you literally get more ice cream – even though the container may be the same size as the cheaper versions. If you have ever let cheap ice cream melt completely, you'll notice there ain't a lot of ice cream in the bottom of your bowl, because all the air has gone away.

With these super-healthy recipes, the goal is to get as close to that dense, creamy texture of traditional ice creams as we can, so we want to incorporate as little air as possible during mixing. Traditional ice creams have you stirring slowly in a pan to make the custard base. These recipes use a blender, and blenders add air.

Then along comes our friend, guar gum. Guar gum makes the ice cream custard into an emulsion – which is a very wonderful thing – but once an emulsion is formed, air gets trapped faster and more easily than ever. We don't want that. Whey powder and powdered egg whites have a similar effect, although to a lesser degree.

So now you know what the goal is, and why, here are your mixing tips and tricks:

- Blend for as short a time as possible just to mix the ingredients together. When the recipe says 10 seconds, it means no more than 10 seconds. Counting is your friend.
- Blend on as low a speed as possible to get the job done. Higher speed = more air whipped in.
- Always add the whey protein or powdered egg whites at the end, and only blend just long enough to mix them in.
- Always add the guar gum last. Tap the gum into the mixture through the opening in the lid while the blender is running and then turn it off.
- Do not over blend, especially once you have added the whey or powdered egg whites, and the guar gum.
- Leave the ice cream custard to rest overnight in the 'fridge if you can possibly stand it. Not only does this allow the custard to get super-cold (very important for churning) but it also allows air to escape from the custard.
- Just before pouring the custard into the churner, gently and slowly stir the custard with a spatula to help eliminate more trapped air bubbles.

Churning and Freezing

As with mixing, churning adds air. Churning incorporates less air, less quickly than mixing because it churns at a much slower speed, and the churner has wide paddles rather than skinny blades like a blender.

Churning encourages the ice cream custard to form small ice crystals instead of large ones as it freezes. Churning also enables the ice cream to freeze uniformly. The faster your ice cream freezes in the churner, the better texture your final frozen ice cream will be.

The goal is to churn your ice cream custard in as short a time as possible, so you incorporate the least amount of air, and so that the ice cream does not have time to make large ice crystals. Give ice crystals an inch and they take a mile.

Your biggest aid in this churning endeavor is having everything super cold before you begin.

Here are your churning and freezing tips and tricks:

- If you live in a hot climate – or if it's just a hot day where you are – churn in the coolest part of the day, and in the coolest room in the house. Have the A/C on. Have the fans on. Think cool.
- If you are using a churner with a removable freezer bowl that needs to be pre-frozen, make sure that it is completely frozen before you churn. If you shake it and there is ANY noise, it is not ready to use. Overnight is typically sufficient to freeze the bowl.
- Your ice cream custard needs to be *really* cold before you churn it. To be really cold it needs to be refrigerated for at least 8 hours, and preferably overnight. DO NOT TRY AND CHURN THE ICE CREAM CUSTARD IF IT IS NOT COLD. All that will happen is that it will churn for so long that the freezer bowl starts to defrost and then all you are doing is incorporating air into custard that is not getting frozen. You will be sad.
- All your equipment should be as cold as possible before you start churning: the dasher (stirring paddle), any jug that you use to pour the custard into the churner, and the spatulas.
- Do not get the freezer bowl out of the freezer until you are ready to use it straight away.
- Do not assume that the custard you make from one of these recipes will all fit in your churner in one batch. There are too many variables for me to be able to produce recipes that are exactly the right quantity for every churner available. Be prepared to churn in two batches at times. Unless you allow your freezer bowl to defrost completely, you will be able to churn the second batch very quickly after the first. Just make sure that you rinse (in cold water) the freezer bowl, and get it back in the freezer as fast as possible once you have removed the first batch of churned ice cream.
- Do not overfill the churning bowl with ice cream custard. Ice cream increases in volume as it churns since air is being incorporated. If you overfill the churner the ice cream will take too long to freeze, will churn for too long, and you'll have a big mess as it starts coming out of the top of the churner. None of these are desirable outcomes. Doing two smaller batches is much better than trying to churn too big a batch.

- These ice cream recipes typically take longer to churn than traditional ice creams, and they are also softer when churned. If you have churned traditional ice cream this may throw you until you get used to it. These ice creams do not churn to more than soft-serve consistency. They finish freezing in the deep freeze.
- Place the empty container that you are going to put the churned ice cream into, in the freezer when you start churning so it is super-cold when the ice cream has churned.
- Once you have put the churned ice cream in the cold storage container, place it in the deep freezer immediately.
- If you have a separate "deep" freeze, put your freshly churned ice cream in that freezer initially, so it freezes as fast and firm as possible. The next day you can transfer it to the freezer part of your kitchen 'fridge/freezer.
- Once churned, freeze the ice cream in the deep freezer for at least 8 hours before serving, and preferably overnight. Really, try and wait, or churn just before bedtime so you're not tempted to dig in straight away.

Once your ice cream has completely frozen, it is ready to scoop and eat – finally!

Here's a few final points to note about these ice creams that is different to traditional ice creams:

- The use of guar gum as an emulsifier creates an ice cream that is less dense than traditional home-made ice cream, so they have a tendency to melt faster once they are out of the deep freeze. Bear this is in mind when you are getting ready to serve your ice cream. They do not need to be taken out of the freezer ahead of time like many premium ice creams do.
- Do not keep your ice cream out of the freezer any longer than is necessary. Once you have scooped, get the ice cream container back in the freezer as fast as you can.
- They do not travel as well as traditional ice creams because they melt faster.
- Once melted, they cannot be re-frozen successfully.
- Once melted, they cannot be re-churned successfully.

Now, let's get in the kitchen and get our ice cream on!

RECIPES: CHOCOLATES, COFFEES, AND VANILLAS

See also:

Va-va-voom Vanilla

1 cup / 8 fl oz. almond milk, unsweetened vanilla

1 whole vanilla pod, split lengthwise and the seeds scraped out

3 ½ oz. / 100g xylitol

1 tsp. sea salt

½ cup / 4 fl oz. heavy (double) cream

1 ½ cups / 12 fl oz. thick coconut milk

1 tsp. vanilla extract

2 ½ oz. / 75g vanilla 100% whey protein powder

½ tsp. guar gum

Warm the almond milk, vanilla seeds and pod, xylitol, sea salt, and cream in a medium pan until it just starts to boil. Remove from the heat, cover and leave for an hour to steep.

Pour the vanilla-infused milk through a sieve to remove the vanilla pod.

Place the thick coconut milk in a blender with the vanilla-infused milk, and the vanilla extract, and blend for 10 seconds.

Turn the blender to low speed, and while the blender is running, add the whey protein powder, then the guar gum, through the opening in the lid, and blend for 5 seconds. Do not over blend.

Pour the ice cream mix into a bowl, cover, and place in the 'fridge for at least 8 hours, preferably overnight.

Read the churning and freezing section on page 23, and freeze the ice cream in your churner according to the manufacturer's instructions. It typically takes between 20 – 30 minutes to freeze.

Once the ice cream has frozen to a soft-serve consistency, quickly transfer it from the churning bowl into your pre-chilled container, and place in the freezer for at least 8 hours, preferably overnight.

~~~~~~

If I'm honest, vanilla ice cream never really floated my boat growing up. The use of real, live vanilla pods crammed full of tiny, heavily-scented specks of deliciousness sure changed my mind on the whole darn vanilla-is-dull thing. Will you just look at all those adorable little black speckles? I still won't choose a dish of vanilla on its own, but it is a heaven-sent addition to any number of other desserts, or simple bowl of ripe, fresh berries. Yay, vanilla pods!

Charismatic Coffee

1 cup / 8 fl oz. almond milk, unsweetened vanilla

5 ¼ oz. / 150g whole coffee beans

5 ¼ oz. / 150g xylitol

1 tsp. sea salt

½ cup / 4 fl oz. heavy (double) cream

1 ½ cups / 12 fl oz. thick coconut milk

1 TBSP whole coffee beans, finely ground

1 tsp. vanilla extract

2 ½ oz. / 75g vanilla 100% whey protein powder

½ tsp. guar gum

In a pan, bring the almond milk, whole coffee beans, xylitol, sea salt, and cream to the boil over a medium heat. Stir. Remove from the heat, cover and leave to steep for an hour.

Strain the coffee-infused mixture through a sieve to remove the beans.

Place the thick coconut milk into a blender, and add the coffee-infused milk, the ground coffee, and the vanilla extract, and blend for 10 seconds.

Turn the blender to low speed, and while the blender is running, add the whey protein powder, then the guar gum, through the opening in the lid, and blend for 5 seconds. Do not over blend.

Pour the ice cream mix into a bowl, cover, and place in the 'fridge for at least 8 hours, preferably overnight.

Read the churning and freezing section on page 23, and freeze the ice cream in your churner according to the manufacturer's instructions. It typically takes between 20 – 30 minutes to freeze.

Once the ice cream has frozen to a soft-serve consistency, quickly transfer it from the churning bowl into your pre-chilled container, and place in the freezer for at least 8 hours, preferably overnight.

Note: because of the extra sweetener required for this flavor, the ice cream does not freeze as hard as most. If you can store it in a deep freezer instead of your 'fridge / freezer, I would recommend that you do so. Be very fast when taking it out of the freezer to serve.

~~~~~~

Your kitchen will smell like a coffee roasters by the time you're done steeping. Just saying.

Dazzling Double Dark Chocolate

1 ½ cups / 12 fl oz. hemp milk, unsweetened original

½ cup / 4 fl oz. heavy (double) cream

5 ¼ oz. / 150g xylitol

½ tsp. sea salt

1 ¼ oz. / 35g raw, unsweetened cocoa powder

2 oz. / 55g 100% cocoa solids chocolate (unsweetened), chopped

1 ½ cups / 12 fl oz. thick coconut milk

1 tsp. vanilla extract

2 ½ oz. / 75g vanilla 100% whey protein powder

½ tsp. guar gum

Place the hemp milk, cream, xylitol, sea salt, and cocoa powder in a pan over medium heat and whisk until the cocoa powder is completely mixed in. Bring to the boil, reduce the heat, and simmer for 1 minute, whisking constantly.

Remove pan from the heat and stir in the chopped chocolate.

Leave to cool, stirring well occasionally.

Place the thick coconut milk and vanilla extract in the blender, add the cooled chocolate custard and blend for 10 seconds.

Turn the blender to low speed, and while the blender is running, add the whey protein powder, then the guar gum, through the opening in the lid, and blend for 5 seconds. Do not over blend.

Pour the ice cream mix into a bowl, cover, and place in the 'fridge for at least 8 hours, preferably overnight.

Read the churning and freezing section on page 23, and freeze the ice cream in your churner according to the manufacturer's instructions. It typically takes between 20 – 30 minutes to freeze.

Once the ice cream has frozen to a soft-serve consistency, quickly transfer it from the churning bowl into your pre-chilled container, and place in the freezer for at least 8 hours, preferably overnight.

~~~~~~

Chocolate Ice Cream how it ought to be: deep, dark, and decidedly delicious. And good for you.

Vivacious Vanilla Pear Hazelnut

Pear Sauce (recipe page 97) – this needs to be made in advance

4 oz / 110g hazelnuts

1 cup / 8 fl oz. almond milk, unsweetened vanilla

3 ½ oz. / 100g xylitol

1 tsp. sea salt

½ cup / 4 fl oz. heavy (double) cream

1 ½ cups / 12 fl oz. thick coconut milk

1 tsp. vanilla extract

2 ½ oz. / 75g vanilla 100% whey protein powder

½ tsp. guar gum

Prepare the Pear Sauce. Store in an airtight container in the 'fridge until churning time.

Toast the hazelnuts under a broiler (grill) until golden brown. It happens fast – don't leave!

Careful turn the hot hazelnuts onto a clean kitchen towel on the counter. Place another clean kitchen towel over the nuts and rub them hard to remove the papery, brown skins. Discard the skins and leave the nuts to cool. Chop the nuts roughly and store in an airtight container.

Place all remaining ingredients EXCEPT the whey protein powder and guar gum in a blender and blend for 10 seconds.

Turn the blender to low speed, and while the blender is running, add the whey protein powder, then the guar gum, through the opening in the lid, and blend for 5 seconds. Do not over blend.

Pour the ice cream mix into a bowl, cover, and place in the 'fridge for at least 8 hours, preferably overnight.

Read the churning and freezing section on page 23, and freeze the ice cream in your churner according to the manufacturer's instructions. It typically takes between 20 – 30 minutes to freeze.

Once the ice cream has frozen to a soft-serve consistency in the churner, pour the chopped nuts through the opening in the top of the churner and churn until mixed through.

Once the nuts are mixed through, quickly spoon a layer of ice cream into the bottom of your cold storage container. Spoon large dollops of Pear Sauce over the ice cream, and then continue to layer ice cream and pear sauce until the ice cream has all been removed from the churner. Be careful to 'dollop' the ice cream layer over the Pear Sauce so that there is as little movement of the sauce as possible. Otherwise you will get 'muddy' ice cream.

Mighty Moose Tracks

1 cup / 8 fl oz. almond milk, unsweetened vanilla

5 ¼ oz. / 100g xylitol

1 tsp. sea salt

½ cup / 4 fl oz. heavy (double) cream

1 ½ cups / 12 fl oz. thick coconut milk

2 tsp. vanilla extract

3 oz. / 85g powdered egg white

½ tsp. guar gum

Chocolate Fudge Ripple (recipe page 99) – this needs to be made in advance

Peanut Butter Drops (recipe page 104) – this needs to be made in advance

Place all ingredients EXCEPT the powdered egg whites and guar gum in a blender, and blend for 10 seconds.

Turn the blender to low speed, and while the blender is running, add the powdered egg whites, then the guar gum, through the opening in the lid, and blend for 5 seconds. Do not over blend.

Pour the ice cream mix into a bowl, cover, and place in the 'fridge for at least 8 hours, preferably overnight.

Read the churning and freezing section on page 23, and freeze the ice cream in your churner according to the manufacturer's instructions. It typically takes between 20 – 30 minutes to freeze.

Once the ice cream has frozen to a soft-serve consistency in the churner, quickly spoon a layer of ice cream into the bottom of your cold storage container. Spoon large dollops of Chocolate Fudge Ripple over the ice cream, then sprinkle Peanut Butter Drops on top. Continue to layer ice cream, Fudge Ripple, and Peanut Butter Drops until the ice cream has all been removed from the churner. Be careful to 'dollop' the ice cream layer over the Fudge Ripple so that there is as little movement of the fudge ripple as possible. Otherwise you will get 'muddy' ice cream.

Place in the deep freezer for at least 8 hours, preferably overnight.

~~~~~~

I've always loved moose. I once saw 6 moose in the wild up in Canada one winter, and I was so excited I nearly fell out of the truck. I'm not entirely sure what the fudge ripple and peanut butter drops have to do with moose, but this stuff sure tastes good.

Cheeky Chocolate Peanut Butter

1 ½ cups / 12 fl oz. hemp milk, unsweetened original

½ cup / 4 fl oz. heavy (double) cream

5 ¼ oz. / 150g xylitol

½ tsp. sea salt

1 ¼ oz. / 35g raw, unsweetened cocoa powder

1 ½ cups / 12 fl oz. thick coconut milk

1 tsp. vanilla extract

3 oz. / 85g powdered egg white

½ tsp. guar gum

Peanut Butter Drops (recipe page 104) – this needs to be made in advance

Place the hemp milk, cream, xylitol, sea salt, and cocoa powder in a pan over medium heat and whisk until the cocoa powder is completely mixed in. Bring to the boil, reduce the heat, and simmer for 1 minute, whisking constantly.

Leave to cool stirring well occasionally. Do not be tempted to work with the chocolate milk while it is still hot – you will cook the egg whites and there will be no ice cream.

Place the thick coconut milk and vanilla extract in the blender, add the cooled chocolate custard and blend for 10 seconds.

Turn the blender to low speed, and while the blender is running, add the powdered egg whites, then the guar gum, through the opening in the lid, and blend for 5 seconds. Do not over blend.

Pour the ice cream mix into a bowl, cover, and place in the 'fridge for at least 8 hours, preferably overnight.

Read the churning and freezing section on page 23, and freeze the ice cream in your churner according to the manufacturer's instructions. It typically takes between 20 – 30 minutes to freeze.

Once the ice cream has frozen to a soft-serve consistency in the churner, quickly spoon a layer of ice cream into the bottom of your cold storage container. Sprinkle Peanut Butter Drops over the ice cream, and then continue to layer ice cream and Peanut Butter Drops until the ice cream has all been removed from the churner.

~~~~~~

Peanut Butter is awesome. That's all I have to say on the matter.

Jiving Java Choc Chip

1 cup / 8 fl oz. almond milk, unsweetened vanilla

6 oz. / 170g whole coffee beans

5 ¼ oz. / 150g xylitol

1 tsp. sea salt

½ cup / 4 fl oz. heavy (double) cream

1 ½ cups / 12 fl oz. thick coconut milk

1 tsp. vanilla extract

2 ½ oz. / 75g vanilla 100% whey protein powder

½ tsp. guar gum

2 oz. / 55g cocoa nibs

In a pan, bring the almond milk, whole coffee beans, xylitol, sea salt and cream to the boil over a medium heat. Stir. Remove from the heat, cover and leave to steep for an hour.

Strain the coffee-infused milk through a sieve to remove the beans.

Place the thick coconut milk into a blender with the coffee-infused milk, and the vanilla extract, and blend for 10 seconds.

Turn the blender to low speed, and while the blender is running, add the whey protein powder, then the guar gum, through the opening in the lid, and blend for 5 seconds. Do not over blend.

Pour the ice cream mix into a bowl, cover, and place in the 'fridge for at least 8 hours, preferably overnight.

Read the churning and freezing section on page 23, and freeze the ice cream in your churner according to the manufacturer's instructions. It typically takes between 20 – 30 minutes to freeze.

Once the ice cream has frozen to a soft-serve consistency in the churner, pour the cocoa nibs through the opening in the top of the churner and churn until mixed through.

Quickly transfer the ice cream from the churning bowl into your pre-chilled container, and place in the deep freezer for at least 8 hours, preferably overnight.

Note: because of the extra sweetener required for this flavor, the ice cream does not freeze as hard as most. If you can store it in a deep freezer instead of your 'fridge / freezer, I would recommend that you do so. Be very fast when taking it out of the freezer to serve.

~~~~~~

Resplendent Rocky Road

1 ½ cups / 12 fl oz. hemp milk, unsweetened original

½ cup / 4 fl oz. heavy (double) cream

5 ¼ oz. / 150g xylitol

½ tsp. sea salt

1 ¼ oz. / 35g raw, unsweetened cocoa powder

1 ½ cups / 12 fl oz. thick coconut milk

1 tsp. vanilla extract

3 oz. / 85g powdered egg white

½ tsp. guar gum

3 oz. / 85g walnuts, toasted and chopped

Sugar-free Marshmallows (recipe page 105) – these need to be made in advance

Place the hemp milk, cream, xylitol, sea salt, and cocoa powder in a pan over medium heat and whisk until the cocoa powder is completely mixed in. Bring to the boil, reduce the heat, and simmer for 1 minute, whisking constantly.

Leave to cool stirring well occasionally. Do not be tempted to work with the chocolate milk while it is still hot – you will cook the egg whites and there will be no ice cream.

Place the thick coconut milk and vanilla extract in the blender, add the cooled chocolate custard and blend for 10 seconds.

Turn the blender to low speed, and while the blender is running, add the powdered egg whites, then the guar gum, through the opening in the lid, and blend for 5 seconds. Do not over blend.

Pour the ice cream mix into a bowl, cover, and place in the 'fridge for at least 8 hours, preferably overnight.

Read the churning and freezing section on page 23, and freeze the ice cream in your churner according to the manufacturer's instructions. It typically takes between 20 – 30 minutes to freeze.

Once the ice cream has frozen to a soft-serve consistency in the churner, quickly spoon a layer of ice cream into the bottom of your cold storage container. Sprinkle toasted walnuts and marshmallows over the ice cream, and then continue to layer ice cream, walnuts, and marshmallows until the ice cream has all been removed from the churner.

Place in the deep freezer for at least 8 hours, preferably overnight.

Amazing Coffee Almond Fudge

1 cup / 8 fl oz. hemp milk, unsweetened vanilla

3 ½ oz. / 100g whole coffee beans

4 ½ oz. / 125g xylitol

1 tsp. sea salt

½ cup / 4 fl oz. heavy (double) cream

1 ½ cups / 12 fl oz. thick coconut milk

1 tsp. vanilla extract

2 ½ oz. / 75g vanilla 100% whey protein powder

½ tsp. guar gum

4 oz. / 110g slivered almonds, toasted

Chocolate Fudge Ripple (recipe page 99) – this needs to be made in advance

In a pan, bring the hemp milk, whole coffee beans, xylitol, sea salt, and cream to the boil over a medium heat. Stir. Remove from the heat, cover and leave to steep for an hour.

Strain the coffee-infused milk through a sieve to remove the beans. (Dry the beans overnight, grind them finely, and then use them to fertilize your roses. BEST. ROSES. EVER.)

Place the thick coconut milk, coffee-infused milk, and the vanilla extract into a blender. Blend for 10 seconds.

Turn the blender to low speed, and while the blender is running, add the whey protein powder, then the guar gum, through the opening in the lid, and blend for 5 seconds. Do not over blend.

Pour the ice cream mix into a bowl, cover, and place in the 'fridge for at least 8 hours, preferably overnight.

Read the churning and freezing section on page 23, and freeze the ice cream in your churner according to the manufacturer's instructions. It typically takes between 20 – 30 minutes to freeze.

Once the ice cream has frozen to a soft-serve consistency in the churner, add the toasted almonds to the churner through the opening in the top, and churn until mixed through.

Once the nuts are mixed through, quickly spoon a layer of ice cream into the bottom of your cold storage container. Spoon large dollops of Chocolate Fudge Ripple over the ice cream, and then continue to layer ice cream and fudge until the ice cream has all been removed from the churner. Be careful to 'dollop' the ice cream layer over the Fudge Ripple so that there is as little movement of the fudge as possible. Otherwise you will get 'muddy' ice cream.

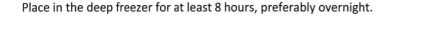

Place in the deep freezer for at least 8 hours, preferably overnight.

~~~~~~

Wondering why the three images of chocolate ice cream in this chapter all look a little different in color from each other, and may look different to other chocolate ice creams you've eaten?

Here's why:

- Different brands of cocoa powders and chocolates are different colors. I use Valrhona cocoa powder which has a lovely red tint to it.

- The recipes are different. One has 100% chocolate in it as well as cocoa powder, which makes the ice cream darker. I lightened the base chocolate recipes for the Resplendent Rocky Road and Cheeky Chocolate Peanut Butter to allow the flavor of the mix-ins to shine through more, instead of them competing with an intense chocolate flavor. You could use the Dazzling Double Dark Chocolate base with the mix-ins if you prefer.

- The images were all shot at different times, and light changes everything, including how we perceive colors. An overcast day vs. a bright sunny day can make colors look significantly different.

Talking of chocolate, I spent a couple of years of my life working as a Chocolatier – long before I wised up to the whole sugar-is-making-you-sick thing. I would spend days up to my elbows in thick, dark, molten chocolate while making handmade chocolates in Perth, Australia, and later in London. I also spent time as a Chocolate Sales Rep – extoling the virtues of Valrhona to all the top chefs and retail stores far and wide across England. It was all chocolate, all the time back then; including as much great chocolate as I could eat. Ah, that was the life. Eating chocolate, talking about chocolate, smiling a lot, and getting paid for it.

If you're a lover of this studly bean, you'll be stoked to know that cocoa is all sorts of good for you, just as long as it comes without the sugar. I won't bore you with all the technical geekery, but just know that it is a fabulous source of healthy fats, as well as containing fiber, protein, and bucket loads of minerals and vitamins. Plus, as every woman who has reached child-bearing age knows, chocolate literally makes you happy. Hand over the chocolate and no one gets hurt.

For other delicious recipes using just the cocoa and none of the sugar, head over to www.carriebrown.com, click on the recipes link, and then click on 'Chocolate' in the list of Topics.

RECIPES: FRUITS

See also:

Remarkable Raspberry

18 oz. / 500g fresh or frozen raspberries

1 ½ cups / 12 fl oz. thick coconut milk

1 cup / 8 fl oz. almond milk, unsweetened vanilla

1 cup / 8 fl oz. heavy (double) cream

3 ½ oz. / 100g xylitol

1 tsp. sea salt

2 TBSP lemon juice

2 ½ oz. / 75g vanilla 100% whey protein powder

½ tsp. guar gum

Heat raspberries in a pan over a medium heat until they are very soft – about 15 minutes.

Press the raspberry pulp through a sieve to remove all the seeds. This will take a little while, but will be SO worth the effort! DO NOT puree the raspberries before you sieve them to save you a few minutes because you will end up with a "dusty" taste in the final ice cream. True story.

Place the raspberry puree, thick coconut milk, almond milk, cream, xylitol, sea salt, and lemon juice into a blender and blend for 10 seconds.

Turn the blender to low speed, and while the blender is running, add the whey protein powder, then the guar gum, through the opening in the lid, and blend for 5 seconds. Do not over blend.

Pour the ice cream mix into a bowl, cover, and place in the 'fridge for at least 8 hours, preferably overnight.

Read the churning and freezing section on page 23, and freeze the ice cream in your churner according to the manufacturer's instructions. It typically takes between 20 – 30 minutes to freeze.

Once the ice cream has frozen to a soft-serve consistency, quickly transfer it from the churning bowl into your pre-chilled container, and place in the freezer for at least 8 hours, preferably overnight.

~~~~~~

In honor of the first ice cream I ever made, this was a no-brainer flavor for a spot in this book. I still remember the sheer delight of dishing up that first scoop of raspberry scrumptiousness, and feeling like a 3-year-old jumping in mud puddles as the "Yums!" ran around the table.

Astonishing Apricot Cardamom

8 oz. / 225g fresh apricots, stoned

1 cup / 8 fl oz. almond milk, unsweetened vanilla

½ cup / 4 fl oz. heavy (double) cream

3 ½ oz. / 100g xylitol

½ tsp. sea salt

1 cup / 8 fl oz. thick coconut milk

¾ tsp. ground cardamom

2 ½ oz. / 75g vanilla 100% whey protein powder

½ tsp. guar gum

8 oz. / 225g fresh apricots, stoned and chopped into small pieces

1 oz. / 30g xylitol

Simmer 8 oz. / 225g apricots, almond milk, cream, 3 ½ oz. / 100g xylitol and salt over medium heat until apricots are very soft.

Blend the apricot mixture on high until completely smooth and then press through a fine mesh sieve.

Place the thick coconut milk and ground cardamom in the blender, add the apricot puree and blend for 10 seconds.

Turn the blender to low speed, and while the blender is running, add the whey protein powder, then the guar gum, through the opening in the lid, and blend for 5 seconds. Do not over blend.

Pour the ice cream mix into a bowl, cover, and place in the 'fridge for at least 8 hours, preferably overnight.

At least an hour before churning, mix the remaining 8 oz. / 225g chopped apricots in a bowl with 1 oz. / 30g xylitol and stir well. Leave to marinate, stirring often.

Read the churning and freezing section on page 23, and freeze the ice cream in your churner according to the manufacturer's instructions. It typically takes between 20 – 30 minutes to freeze.

Once the ice cream has frozen to a soft-serve consistency, carefully pour the chopped apricots into the churner and continue churning until mixed through.

Quickly transfer the ice cream from the churning bowl into your pre-chilled container, and place in the freezer for at least 8 hours, preferably overnight.

Perky Pear Poppy Seed

18 oz. / 500g ripe pears, cored

6 tsp. lemon juice

1 cup / 8 fl oz. heavy (double) cream

1 ½ cups / 12 fl oz. thick coconut milk

½ tsp. sea salt

3 ½ oz. / 100g xylitol

2 ½ oz. / 75g vanilla 100% whey protein powder

1 ½ TBSP poppy seeds

1 tsp. guar gum

Place the pears (skin included!) and lemon juice in a blender and blend on high speed until the pears are completely smooth.

Press the pears through a sieve, and discard any fibers.

Place the pear puree, cream, thick coconut milk, sea salt, and xylitol in the blender and blend for 10 seconds.

Turn the blender to low speed, and while the blender is running, add the whey protein powder, the poppy seeds, then the guar gum, through the opening in the lid, and blend for 5 seconds. Do not over blend.

Pour the ice cream mix into a bowl, cover, and place in the 'fridge for at least 8 hours, preferably overnight.

Read the churning and freezing section on page 23, and freeze the ice cream in your churner according to the manufacturer's instructions. It typically takes between 20 – 30 minutes to freeze.

Once the ice cream has frozen to a soft-serve consistency, quickly transfer it from the churning bowl into your pre-chilled container, and place in the deep freezer for at least 8 hours, preferably overnight.

~~~~~~

Oh, pears. You seem so sweet, and innocent, but – truth be told – you were a bit of a bugger to get creamy and scoop-able, and still taste like pear. But we persevered. And got through a truckload of pears. You were totally worth the effort though. And the cursing.

Magnificent Mango Ginger

10 oz. / 280g fresh or frozen mango flesh

3 ½ oz. / 100g xylitol

1 tsp. sea salt

1 ½ tsp. lime juice

1 ½ cups / 12 fl oz. thick coconut milk

½ cup thin coconut milk

½ tsp. ground ginger

2 ½ oz. / 75g vanilla 100% whey protein powder

½ tsp. guar gum

Place the mango, xylitol, sea salt, and lime juice in a pan and cook over medium heat until the mango is very soft.

Blend the mango mixture on high speed until completely smooth and then press through a sieve. Discard any mango fibers.

Place the mango puree, thick coconut milk, thin coconut milk, and ground ginger in the blender and blend for 10 seconds.

Turn the blender to low speed, and while the blender is running, add the whey protein powder, then the guar gum, through the opening in the lid, and blend for 5 seconds. Do not over blend.

Pour the ice cream mix into a bowl, cover, and place in the 'fridge for at least 8 hours, preferably overnight.

Read the churning and freezing section on page 23, and freeze the ice cream in your churner according to the manufacturer's instructions. It typically takes between 20 – 30 minutes to freeze.

Once the ice cream has frozen to a soft-serve consistency, quickly transfer it from the churning bowl into your pre-chilled container, and place in the freezer for at least 8 hours, preferably overnight.

~~~~~~

I once toured the Buderim Ginger Factory in Queensland, Australia. It was awesome. It seems there's no end to the fantastical stuff you can do with ginger; all of them good. Including adding it to Mango Ice Cream. It's incredible what a pinch of spice can do to take a recipe from ordinary to other-worldly. And you don't even need to own a space shuttle.

Brilliant Blueberry Cheesecake

8 oz. / 225g full fat cream cheese

Zest of 1 lemon

1 cup / 8 fl oz. non-fat sour cream

1 tsp. sea salt

4 ½ oz. / 125g xylitol

½ cup / 4 fl oz. almond milk, unsweetened vanilla

½ tsp. lemon extract

2 ½ oz. / 75g vanilla 100% whey protein powder

Blueberry Sauce (recipe page 96)

Place the cream cheese, lemon zest, sour cream, sea salt, xylitol, almond milk, and lemon extract into a blender and blend for 10 seconds.

Turn the blender to low speed, and while the blender is running, add the whey protein powder through the opening in the lid, and blend for 5 seconds. Do not over blend.

Pour the ice cream mix into a bowl, cover, and place in the 'fridge for at least 8 hours, preferably overnight.

Read the churning and freezing section on page 23, and freeze the ice cream in your churner according to the manufacturer's instructions. It typically takes between 20 – 30 minutes to freeze.

Once the ice cream has frozen to a soft-serve consistency, quickly spoon a layer of ice cream into the bottom of your cold storage container. Spoon dollops of Blueberry Sauce over the ice cream, and then continue to layer ice cream and blueberry sauce until the ice cream has all been removed from the churner. Be careful to dollop the ice cream and not stir. You don't want "muddy" ice cream.

Place in the deep freezer for at least 8 hours, preferably overnight.

~~~~~~

Forrest: holy $#@% that's good.

Forrest: Seriously. Eric and I are supposed to be discussing sales quotas...and we're just staring at each other.

CB: :-)

Forrest: Yes – like that. :->> more like that. All hopped up on delicious.

Marvelous Mango Sorbet

2 lb / 900g fresh or frozen mango flesh

⅔ cup / 5 ½ fl oz. water

4 ½ oz. / 125g xylitol

1 tsp. sea salt

6 tsp. lime juice

1 TBSP rum

Place the mango, water, xylitol, sea salt, lime juice, and rum in a blender and blend on high until smooth.

Press the mango puree through a fine mesh sieve into a bowl. Discard any fibers left in the sieve.

Cover the sorbet, and place in the 'fridge for at least 8 hours, preferably overnight.

Read the churning and freezing section on page 23, and freeze the sorbet in your churner according to the manufacturer's instructions. It typically takes between 20 – 30 minutes to freeze.

Once the sorbet has frozen to a soft-serve consistency, quickly transfer it from the churning bowl into your pre-chilled container, and place in the freezer for at least 8 hours, preferably overnight.

~~~~~~

Oh my goodness! How easy was that? But wait! Here's some tips to make it even easier!

Sneaky money-saving tip: buy frozen mango pieces. Just check there's nothing but mango.

Sneaky time-saving tip: buy frozen mango pieces. Just check there's nothing but mango.

Sneaky labor-saving tip: buy frozen mango pieces. Just check there's nothing but mango.

Sneaky waste-saving tip: buy frozen mango pieces. Just check there's nothing but mango.

Spectacular Orange Spice

½ cup / 4 fl oz. heavy (double) cream

1 tsp. sea salt

5 ¼ oz. / 150g xylitol

Zest ½ orange

12 oz. / 335g orange flesh, peeled

1 ½ cups / 12 fl oz. thick coconut milk

2 tsp. ground coriander

½ tsp. ground cloves

½ tsp. vanilla extract

½ cup / 4 fl oz. pasteurized egg whites

½ tsp. guar gum

Warm the cream, sea salt, and xylitol in a pan until it just starts to boil. Remove from heat, zest the orange directly into the cream, stir, cover, and steep for an hour.

Sieve the orange cream to remove the orange zest. Do not leave the orange zest in! It makes the ice cream bitter. Ignore this at your peril.

Place the orange-infused cream, orange flesh, thick coconut milk, ground coriander, ground cloves, vanilla extract, and egg whites in the blender and blend for 10 seconds.

Turn the blender to low speed, and while the blender is running, add the guar gum through the opening in the lid, and blend for 5 seconds. Do not over blend.

Pour the ice cream mix into a bowl, cover, and place in the 'fridge for at least 8 hours, preferably overnight.

Read the churning and freezing section on page 23, and freeze the ice cream in your churner according to the manufacturer's instructions. It typically takes between 20 – 30 minutes to freeze.

Once the ice cream has frozen to a soft-serve consistency, quickly transfer it from the churning bowl into your pre-chilled container, and place in the freezer for at least 8 hours, preferably overnight.

~~~~~~

This tastes like Christmas. Or Thanksgiving. I still get confused by the two. They both involve turkey, poinsettias, and loads of people gobbling up loads of food. It's an easy mistake.

Lovely Lemon Meringue Pie

Zest of one lemon

1 cup / 8 fl oz. heavy (double) cream

2 ¼ oz. / 65g xylitol

½ tsp. sea salt

2 cups / 16 fl oz. Lemon Curd (recipe page 101) – this needs to be made in advance

½ cup / 4 fl oz. non-fat Greek yogurt

1 ¾ oz. / 50 g powdered egg whites

½ tsp. guar gum

Sugar-free Meringue Cookies (recipe page 107) – this needs to be made in advance

Lemon Shortbread Cookies (recipe page 103) – this needs to be made in advance

Zest the lemon directly into a small pan.

Add the cream, xylitol, and sea salt to the pan with the lemon zest, stir well, and heat until bubbles just start to break the surface. Remove from the heat, cover and leave to cool.

Sieve the cooled lemon cream to remove the lemon zest. Discard the zest.

Place the lemon cream in a blender with the Lemon Curd and yogurt, and blend for 10 seconds.

Turn the blender to low speed, and while the blender is running, add the powdered egg whites, then the guar gum, through the opening in the lid, and blend for 5 seconds. Do not over blend.

Pour the ice cream mix into a bowl, cover, and place in the 'fridge for at least 8 hours, preferably overnight.

Read the churning and freezing section on page 23, and freeze the ice cream in your churner according to the manufacturer's instructions. It typically takes between 20 – 30 minutes to freeze.

Once the ice cream has frozen to a soft-serve consistency in the churner, quickly spoon a layer into the bottom of your cold storage container. Sprinkle Meringue Cookies and broken Lemon Shortbread Cookies over the ice cream. Continue to layer ice cream and cookies until the ice cream has all been removed from the churner.

Place in the deep freezer for at least 8 hours, preferably overnight.

~~~~~~

Oh, for the love of all things lemony and delectable, this ice cream is ridiculous.

Perfectly Peaches and Cream

½ cup / 4 fl oz. hemp milk, unsweetened original

10 oz. / 280g fresh peaches, stones removed

1 cup / 8 fl oz. heavy (double) cream

¾ tsp. sea salt

3 ½ oz. / 100g xylitol

1 cup / 8 fl oz. thick coconut milk

2 ½ oz. / 75g vanilla 100% whey protein powder

½ tsp. guar gum

7 oz. / 200g fresh peaches, stones removed and chopped into small pieces

1 oz. / 30g xylitol

Place hemp milk, 10oz / 280g peaches, cream, sea salt, and 3 ½ oz. / 100g xylitol in a pan and simmer over a medium heat until peaches are very soft – about 15 minutes.

Place the peach mixture in a blender and blend until completely smooth.

Pass through a fine sieve to remove any peach fibers.

Place the peach puree and thick coconut milk in the blender and blend for 10 seconds.

Turn the blender to low speed, and while the blender is running, add the whey protein powder, then the guar gum, through the opening in the lid, and blend for 5 seconds. Do not over blend.

Pour the ice cream mix into a bowl, cover, and place in the 'fridge for at least 8 hours, preferably overnight.

Meanwhile, place the remaining 7 oz. / 200g chopped peaches in a bowl with 1 oz. / 30g xylitol and mix well. Cover and leave to marinate for at least an hour, stirring often.

Read the churning and freezing section on page 23, and freeze the ice cream in your churner according to the manufacturer's instructions. It typically takes between 20 – 30 minutes to freeze.

Once the ice cream has frozen to a soft-serve consistency in the churner, add the marinated peach pieces to the churner and churn until mixed through.

Quickly transfer the ice cream from the churning bowl into your pre-chilled container, and place in the deep freezer for at least 8 hours, preferably overnight.

~~~~~~

Ravishing Raspberry Sorbet

12 oz. / 340g fresh or frozen raspberries

4 ½ oz. / 125g xylitol

2 cups / 16 fl oz. water

Place the raspberries, xylitol, and water in a pan and heat over medium for 10 minutes.

Press the raspberries through a fine mesh sieve to remove all the seeds. This will take a little while, but will be SO worth the effort! DO NOT puree the raspberries before you sieve them to save you a few minutes. You will end up with a "dusty" taste in your sorbet. True story.

Cover the sorbet, and place in the 'fridge for at least 8 hours, preferably overnight.

Read the churning and freezing section on page 23, and freeze the sorbet in your churner according to the manufacturer's instructions. It typically takes between 20 – 30 minutes to freeze.

Once the sorbet has frozen to a soft-serve consistency, quickly transfer it from the churning bowl into your pre-chilled container, and place in the freezer for at least 8 hours, preferably overnight.

~~~~~~

I grew up with raspberries. My father had several established raspberry canes at the bottom of our garden, and those things produced the biggest, juiciest, most flavorful raspberries like nobody's business. By the barrel-load, I might add. Every day in the school holidays I would get to go pick the raspberries, and incredibly, despite the number that got hijacked off on a trip down my gullet, thousands of luscious, bright red berries made their way up to the house and into my mother's kitchen. It was a common occurrence to see me downing a huge slice of raspberry flan for breakfast.

During the summertime, every freezer we opened had a tray of sparkling, red berries lying on trays in neat rows, soon to be piled into containers and stacked fastidiously in the icy depths, ready for jam making, or flan making, or trifle making. Yes, we ate a lot of raspberries.

My favorite way to eat them was to sneak a frozen berry from the open tray just inside the freezer, pop it my mouth, and let it slowly defrost against my tongue, the flavor getting deeper and deeper as the seconds ticked by, until it collapsed in my mouth with a gush of tart juices.

Every time I taste raspberries now I am immediately transported back to Kent – the Garden of England – where my summers were filled with thousands of those beautiful red jewels.

Sassy Spiced Apricot Sherbet

1lb 12oz. / 785g fresh apricots, stones removed

7oz / 200g xylitol

2 tsp. vanilla extract

3 tsp. ground coriander

½ tsp. sea salt

3 ¾ oz. / 105g vanilla 100% whey protein powder

½ tsp. guar gum

Cook the apricots and xylitol in a pan over a medium heat, until the apricots are very soft – about 15 minutes. Stir well.

Press the apricot mixture through a sieve, and discard any fibers.

Place the apricot puree, vanilla extract, ground coriander, and sea salt in a blender and blend for 10 seconds.

With the blender still running on HIGH SPEED, quickly add - through the opening in the lid - the whey protein powder, then the guar gum, and blend for 10 seconds. Your blender may complain – this one is hard work!

Pour the apricot mixture into a bowl, cover, and place in the 'fridge for at least 8 hours, preferably overnight.

Read the churning and freezing section on page 23, and freeze the ice cream in your churner according to the manufacturer's instructions. It typically takes between 20 – 30 minutes to freeze.

Once the sherbet has frozen to a soft-serve consistency, quickly transfer it from the churning bowl into your pre-chilled container, and place in the deep freezer for at least 8 hours, preferably overnight.

~~~~~~

This recipe was a complete, but entirely happy, accident. It started out as a whole pile of apricots with nothing to do. It ended up as a delicious dish of delightful apricot fluff. Let's be clear – it's really not ice cream. It is, however, a magical, intensely fruity frozen dessert that is both light and satiating all at the same time.

I started out by making a spiced apricot puree, and then before I even knew what was going on I got hijacked by Right Brain wondering what would happen if I added a whole bunch of vanilla whey powder and nothing else, and then churned it. This. This is what happens.

Smashing Strawberry

½ cup / 4 fl oz. almond milk, unsweetened vanilla

½ cup / 4 fl oz. heavy (double) cream

½ cup / 4 fl oz. thick coconut milk

1 ¾ oz. / 50g xylitol

½ tsp. sea salt

¼ tsp. vanilla extract

1 ¼ oz. / 35g vanilla 100% whey protein powder

¼ tsp. guar gum

6 oz. / 170g fresh strawberries, roughly chopped

1 oz. / 30g xylitol

Place all ingredients EXCEPT the vanilla 100% whey protein powder and guar gum, in a blender and blend for 10 seconds.

Turn the blender to low speed, and while the blender is running, add the whey protein powder, then the guar gum, through the opening in the lid, and blend for 5 seconds. Do not over blend.

Pour the ice cream mix into a bowl, cover, and place in the 'fridge for at least 8 hours, preferably overnight.

Meanwhile, place the chopped strawberries in a bowl with 1 oz. / 30g xylitol and mix well. Cover and leave to marinate for at least an hour, stirring often. The strawberries will become very juicy. Yum.

Read the churning and freezing section on page 23, and freeze the ice cream in your churner according to the manufacturer's instructions. It typically takes between 20 – 30 minutes to freeze.

Once the ice cream has frozen to a soft-serve consistency in the churner, add the marinated strawberry pieces to the churner and churn until mixed through.

Quickly transfer the ice cream from the churning bowl into your pre-chilled container, and place in the deep freezer for at least 8 hours, preferably overnight.

~~~~~~

This ice cream reminds me of summers in England: Wimbledon, the end of exams, warm, gentle breezes, picnics on the lawn, sunshine, meandering down the banks of the river Thames, roses in full bloom, strolling in Hyde Park, boating in Henley, bowlfuls of fresh strawberries and cream, 7-week-long holidays from school, Mr. Whippy Ice Cream, and Cadbury's flakes. Ah, summer.

Outstanding Orange Creamsicle

Zest of 4 oranges

1 cup / 8 fl oz. almond milk, unsweetened vanilla

½ cup / 4 fl oz. heavy (double) cream

3 ½ oz. / 100g xylitol

½ tsp. sea salt

1 cup / 8 fl oz. thick coconut milk

½ tsp. vanilla extract

1 tsp. orange extract

2 ½ oz. / 75g vanilla whey protein powder

½ tsp. guar gum

Sugar-free Marshmallows (recipe page 105) – these need to be made in advance

Zest the oranges directly into a small pan. Eat the oranges. Or go to my blog – www.carriebrown.com - and get an awesome green smoothie recipe to use them in.

Add the almond milk, cream, xylitol, and sea salt to the pan with the zest, stir well, and bring just to the boil. Remove from the heat, cover, and leave to cool.

Pass the orange milk through a sieve to remove the zest. Discard the zest.

Place the orange milk in a blender with the thick coconut milk, vanilla extract, and orange extract, and blend for 10 seconds.

Turn the blender to low speed, and while the blender is running, add the vanilla whey protein powder, then the guar gum, through the opening in the lid, and blend for 5 seconds. Do not over blend.

Pour the ice cream mix into a bowl, cover, and place in the 'fridge for at least 8 hours, preferably overnight.

Read the churning and freezing section on page 23, and freeze the ice cream in your churner according to the manufacturer's instructions. It typically takes between 20 – 30 minutes to freeze.

Once the ice cream has frozen to a soft-serve consistency in the churner, quickly spoon a layer of ice cream into the bottom of your cold storage container. Sprinkle Marshmallows over the ice cream, and then continue to layer ice cream and Marshmallows until the ice cream has all been removed from the churner.

Place in the deep freezer for at least 8 hours, preferably overnight.

~~~~~~

You may not be counting, but I thought I should mention that there's 10 different ice creams in this little book that involve nuts. That's a third of the book. Unless you count coconut milk in that, in which case it's 30 recipes and the entire book. So let's talk about nuts for a few minutes, because clearly nuts are important. And because really, nuts are stinkin' awesome.

Nuts, nuts, nuts. I've always been a big nut fan. I blame my father. From my mother I inherited a desire to cook, a mind like a steel trap when managing the household budget, a sweet tooth, and a penchant for ironing everything – and I mean *everything* – that comes out of the washing machine. From my father I inherited mad driving skills, silky fine hair, a lifelong fascination with psychotherapy, and a love for nuts.

Over the years I've toasted them, chopped them, ground them, flaked them, and even burnt a few. Except no one likes burnt nuts. I believe I have mentioned that more than a couple of times in these pages. I maintain it is absolutely true.

Growing up, Christmas in England meant piles of nuts – at least at our house. All kinds of nuts from salted peanuts to sugared almonds; and masses of fresh nuts still in their hard, brown winter coats. Every Christmas Eve, out would come the nutcrackers and large wooden bowls brimming with unshelled nuts – brazils, walnuts, cobnuts (hazelnuts), and almonds. As a family we sure put those nutcrackers through their paces, but mostly it was my father and I who took first place in the nut-cracking and devouring stakes. If I had to pick a favorite, though, it wouldn't be hard. Hazelnuts all the way, baby!

Way back when, in London, and Perth, Australia – when I was a professional Chocolatier – as well as being up to my elbows in liquid chocolate every day, I used to roast hazelnuts by hand over an open flame. We were artisans, you know. None of this store-bought pre-roasted debauchery. I'd pile the nuts into a round metal drum and snap shut the little flap on top. The drum then sat on a metal stand which straddled an open flame, and it had a wooden handle at one end. I would sit on a stool and slowly turn that dented, flame-scorched drum by hand until those hazels were a deep, even, golden brown right the way through; by jove those were the best tasting nuts I have ever had the pleasure of popping into my mouth. Then we'd drench them in dark, glistening chocolate. Oh, yes.

These days my hazelnut roasting episodes aren't nearly as winsome or romantic as in times past, but a roasted hazelnut is still a roasted hazelnut when it comes down to the eating. My only issue with roasting hazelnuts is how to not eat them all 4 seconds after they've cooled down. In the Vivacious Vanilla Pear Hazelnut Ice Cream I started out with 4 oz. but there was only 3 oz. left by the time churning commenced. I don't think I can get away with blaming that one on the "kids". Have you ever met a cat that likes roasted hazelnuts?

I rest my case. Guilty as charged.

RECIPES: NUTS

See also:

Bewitching Butter Pecan

1 oz. / 30g butter

5 ¼ oz. / 150g pecan halves

¼ tsp. sea salt

1 cup / 8 fl oz. almond milk, unsweetened vanilla

½ cup / 4 fl oz. heavy (double) cream

3 ½ oz. / 100g xylitol

1 tsp. sea salt

1 tsp. vanilla extract

1 cup / 8 fl oz. thick coconut milk

2 oz. / 55g butter, softened

2 ½ oz. / 75g vanilla 100% whey protein powder

½ tsp. guar gum

Preheat the oven to 350F. Melt the butter in a small pan. Remove from the heat, add the pecans and salt, and stir until the nuts are well coated with butter.

Spread evenly on a baking sheet and toast in the oven for 10 minutes, stirring occasionally, until golden brown. Remove from the oven. Try not to eat them all.

Once the nuts are completely cooled, chop them roughly and store in an airtight container.

Place the almond milk, cream, xylitol, sea salt, vanilla extract, thick coconut milk, and butter in a blender and blend for 10 seconds.

Turn the blender to low speed, and while the blender is running, add the whey protein powder, then the guar gum, through the opening in the lid, and blend for 5 seconds. Do not over blend.

Pour the ice cream mix into a bowl, cover, and place in the 'fridge for at least 8 hours, preferably overnight.

Read the churning and freezing section on page 23, and freeze the ice cream in your churner according to the manufacturer's instructions. It typically takes between 20 – 30 minutes to freeze.

Once the ice cream has frozen to a soft-serve consistency in the churner, add the chopped buttered pecan pieces and churn until mixed through.

Quickly transfer the ice cream from the churning bowl into your pre-chilled container, and place in the deep freezer for at least 8 hours, preferably overnight.

Phenomenal Peanut Butter

2 cups / 16 fl oz. hemp milk, unsweetened original

¾ cup / 6 fl oz. smooth natural unsweetened peanut butter

6 ¼ oz. / 175g xylitol

½ tsp. sea salt

¼ cup / 2 fl oz. heavy (double) cream

¼ tsp. vanilla extract

2 ½ oz. / 75g vanilla 100% whey protein powder

½ tsp. guar gum

Place the hemp milk, peanut butter, xylitol, sea salt, cream, and vanilla extract into a blender and blend for 10 seconds.

Turn the blender to low speed, and while the blender is running, add the whey protein powder, then the guar gum, through the opening in the lid, and blend for 5 seconds. Do not over blend.

Pour the ice cream mix into a bowl, cover, and place in the 'fridge for at least 8 hours, preferably overnight.

Read the churning and freezing section on page 23, and freeze the ice cream in your churner according to the manufacturer's instructions. It typically takes between 20 – 30 minutes to freeze.

Once the ice cream has frozen to a soft-serve consistency, quickly transfer it from the churning bowl into your pre-chilled container, and place in the freezer for at least 8 hours, preferably overnight.

~~~~~~

Here's a few of the comments from my blog about this recipe:

Ellen said, "YUM…..JUST YUM! What an incredible ice cream! LOVE it!! It is DEFINITELY a '5' star recipe!!!"

Suzie said, "Made this ice cream this weekend… It was awesome – way easy to make, the recipe really worked. Thank you Carrie Brown!!! "

Deb said, "Love, love, love this ice cream. Getting ready to make another batch."

I think they liked it, don't you? If you like peanut butter, I think you'll LOVE it.

Tantalizing Toasted Triple Coconut

4 oz. / 110g flaked coconut, unsweetened

1 ½ cups / 12 fl oz. thick coconut milk

1 cup / 8 fl oz. thin coconut milk

3 ½ oz. / 100g xylitol

½ cup / 4 fl oz. heavy (double) cream

1 tsp. sea salt

½ tsp. rum

2 ½ oz. / 75g vanilla 100% whey protein powder

1 tsp. guar gum

Spread the coconut on a baking sheet and toast under a broiler (grill) until lightly browned. Browning happens very quickly – do not walk away! Remove from under the broiler (grill) and leave to cool.

Place 2 oz. / 55g of the toasted coconut, the thick and thin coconut milks, xylitol, cream, sea salt, and rum in a blender and blend for 10 seconds. It will NOT be smooth. DO NOT CONTINUE TO BLEND TO GET TO SMOOTH – it will never happen. Trust me.

Turn the blender to low speed, and while the blender is running, add the whey protein powder, then the guar gum, through the opening in the lid, and blend for 5 seconds. Do not over blend.

Pour the ice cream mix into a bowl, cover, and place in the 'fridge for at least 8 hours, preferably overnight.

Read the churning and freezing section on page 23, and freeze the ice cream in your churner according to the manufacturer's instructions. It typically takes between 20 – 30 minutes to freeze.

Once the ice cream has frozen to a soft-serve consistency in the churner, add the remaining 2 oz. / 55g toasted coconut flakes and churn until mixed through.

Quickly transfer it from the churning bowl into your pre-chilled container, and place in the deep freezer for at least 8 hours, preferably overnight.

~~~~~~

Sneaky emergency rescue tip: Coconut meat can be funny stuff. If you see your ice cream custard looking like it is curdling, add an extra ½ tsp. of guar gum, and whack the blender on high for a few seconds. Oh, and don't panic. It will churn just fine.

Luscious Coconut Lime

3 oz. / 85g flaked or desiccated coconut, unsweetened

Zest of 2 limes

½ cup / 4 fl oz. thin coconut milk, unsweetened

½ cup / 4 fl oz. heavy (double) cream

½ tsp. sea salt

5 ¼ oz. / 150g xylitol

1 ½ cups / 12 fl oz. thick coconut milk, unsweetened

3 oz. / 85g powdered egg white

½ tsp. guar gum

Spread the coconut on a baking sheet and toast under a broiler (grill) until lightly browned. Browning happens very quickly – do not walk away! Remove from under the broiler (grill) and leave to cool.

Zest the limes directly into a small pan.

Add the thin coconut milk, cream, sea salt, and xylitol to the lime zest in the pan and bring just to the boil. Remove from the heat, cover, and leave to cool.

Pass the lime milk through a sieve to remove the zest. Set zest to one side and reserve. You will use it at the churning stage.

Place the lime milk in a blender with the thick coconut milk and toasted coconut, and blend for 10 seconds. It will NOT be smooth. Don't try to make it be smooth!

Turn the blender to low speed, and while the blender is running, add the powdered egg whites, then the guar gum, through the opening in the lid, and blend for 5 seconds. Do not over blend.

Pour the ice cream mix into a bowl, cover, and place in the 'fridge for at least 8 hours, preferably overnight.

Read the churning and freezing section on page 23, and freeze the ice cream in your churner according to the manufacturer's instructions. It typically takes between 20 – 30 minutes to freeze.

Once the ice cream has frozen to a soft-serve consistency in the churner, add the lime zest to the churner through the opening in the top, and churn until mixed through.

Quickly transfer the ice cream from the churning bowl into your pre-chilled container, and place in the deep freezer for at least 8 hours, preferably overnight.

Fantastic Coconut Fudge Chip

3 oz. / 85g flaked or desiccated coconut, unsweetened

1 cup / 8 fl oz. thin coconut milk, unsweetened

½ cup / 4 fl oz. heavy (double) cream

5 ¼ oz. / 150g xylitol

½ tsp. sea salt

1 ½ cups / 12 fl oz. thick coconut milk, unsweetened

3 oz. / 85g powdered egg white

½ tsp. guar gum

1 ¼ oz. / 35g cocoa nibs

Chocolate Fudge Ripple (recipe page 99) – this needs to be made in advance

Spread the coconut on a baking sheet and toast under a broiler (grill) until lightly browned. Browning happens very quickly – do not walk away! Remove from under the broiler (grill) and leave to cool.

Place toasted coconut, thin coconut milk, cream, xylitol, and sea salt, in a pan, and heat until it starts to steam. Remove from the heat, cover, and leave to cool.

Pour the coconut milk through a sieve to remove the toasted coconut. Press hard on the toasted coconut in the sieve to extract as much of the coconut juice as possible. You are not trying to press the coconut through the sieve, just trying to remove maximum amount of juice and flavor from it. Reserve the coconut meat for another use – add it to green smoothies or make the Orange Coconut Cupcakes over at www.carriebrown.com. They are delicious!

Place the pressed coconut milk in a blender with the thick coconut milk, and blend for 10 seconds.

Turn the blender to low speed, and while the blender is running, add the powdered egg whites, then the guar gum, through the opening in the lid, and blend for 5 seconds. Do not over blend.

Pour the ice cream mix into a bowl, cover, and place in the 'fridge for at least 8 hours, preferably overnight.

Read the churning and freezing section on page 23, and freeze the ice cream in your churner according to the manufacturer's instructions. It typically takes between 20 – 30 minutes to freeze.

Once the ice cream has frozen to a soft-serve consistency in the churner, add the cocoa nibs to the churner through the opening in the top, and churn until mixed through.

Once the nibs are mixed through, quickly spoon a layer of ice cream into the bottom of your cold storage container. Spoon large dollops of Chocolate Fudge Ripple over the ice cream, and then continue to layer ice cream and fudge until the ice cream has all been removed from the churner. Be careful to 'dollop" the ice cream layer over the Chocolate Fudge Ripple so that there is as little movement of the fudge as possible. Otherwise you will get 'muddy' ice cream.

Place in the deep freezer for at least 8 hours, preferably overnight.

~~~~~~

If you're wondering why there are 3 different coconut ice creams going on around here, you can mostly blame Jonathan Bailor. Coconut is extraordinarily good for us, and Jonathan never misses an opportunity to remind me of its umpteen virtues. He just loves the stuff. Whenever I create a new recipe for desserts or baked goods, such as cupcakes or cookies, he always grills me on the ingredients, and then follows it up with, "Could you use coconut instead?" So I was pretty clear that if I made coconut ice cream there'd be a huge "Whoop! Whoop!" coming from The Bailornator's corner. If there was ever someone who deserved his own ice cream after all the work he tirelessly does for the health of the world, it would be Jonathan.

The first one I developed was made entirely with Mr. Bailor in mind – the Tantalizing Toasted Triple Coconut – into which I packed as much of that glorious white stuff as I could muster. It is lumpy, bumpy and chock full of tender, juicy coconut meat. If you love ice cream with some serious texture going on, this one's for you.

The second one was inspired by a lovely reader – adding some bright, zesty lime to the proceedings. It also felt rather tropical, a bit like a Piña Colada without the booze. OK, and without the pineapple, but you get the idea. I decided to make this one a little less lumpy and bumpy, but it's still all-coconut, all the time.

The third one I created for all you smooth-and-creamy ice cream lovers. Why should you miss out on all the coconutty goodness just because you don't care for bumpy bits? Except then I turned around and added cocoa nibs. I know, right? But you see, you asked for Coconut Chip Ice Cream, and having 4 coconut ice creams in one book seemed a little much. The good news is that if you really, really just want super-silky, creamy, dreamy coconut ice cream, you can just leave the cocoa nibs out and truly get your smooth on.

Everyone wins!

RECIPES: SPICES, ESSENCES, AND EXTRACTS

Sinless Cinnamon

1 cup / 8 fl oz. almond milk, unsweetened vanilla

½ cup / 4 fl oz. heavy (double) cream

3 ½ oz. / 100g xylitol

½ tsp. sea salt

1 cup / 8 fl oz. thick coconut milk

1 ½ tsp. ground cinnamon

¼ tsp. vanilla extract

2 ½ oz. / 75g vanilla 100% whey protein powder

½ tsp. guar gum

Place the almond milk, cream, xylitol, sea salt, thick coconut milk, ground cinnamon, and vanilla extract into a blender and blend for 10 seconds.

Turn the blender to low speed, and while the blender is running, add the whey protein powder, then the guar gum, through the opening in the lid, and blend for 5 seconds. Do not over blend.

Pour the ice cream mix into a bowl, cover, and place in the 'fridge for at least 8 hours, preferably overnight.

Read the churning and freezing section on page 23, and freeze the ice cream in your churner according to the manufacturer's instructions. It typically takes between 20 – 30 minutes to freeze.

Once the ice cream has frozen to a soft-serve consistency, quickly transfer it from the churning bowl into your pre-chilled container, and place in the freezer for at least 8 hours, preferably overnight.

~~~~~~

The British aren't really Cinnamon Hounds like the Americans are, but I figured that what with the Stars and Stripes Lovers' allegiance to Snickerdoodle Cookies, and their addiction to Cinnamon Rolls, I was probably onto a winner with Cinnamon Ice Cream. During the taste-tests all everyone wanted to know was how I had made ice cream taste like cookies and rolls, which is a really, really good thing if you are gluten-, grain-, and sugar-free and can't eat them live and direct.

To my complete surprise this rose straight into my Top 3 favorite ice cream flavors. Who knew that the girl from Limey Land would one day be swept off her feet by a few dusty brown sticks? America, I think you're onto something.

Miraculous Mint Choc Chip

1 cup / 8 fl oz. thin coconut milk, unsweetened

1 ½ oz. / 40g fresh mint leaves

½ cup / 4 fl oz. heavy (double) cream

½ tsp. sea salt

5 ¼ oz. / 150g xylitol

1 ½ cups / 12 fl oz. thick coconut milk, unsweetened

3 oz. / 85g powdered egg white

½ tsp. guar gum

1 ½ oz. / 45g cocoa nibs

Place thin coconut milk, mint leaves, cream, sea salt, and xylitol in a pan, stir well and bring just to the boil. Remove from the heat, cover and leave to steep for an hour.

Sieve the milk mixture to remove the mint leaves, pressing the mint leaves against the sieve to remove as much flavor as possible.

Place the mint milk and thick coconut milk in the blender and blend for 10 seconds.

Turn the blender to low speed, and while the blender is running, add the powdered egg whites, then the guar gum, through the opening in the lid, and blend for 5 seconds. Do not over blend.

Pour the ice cream mix into a bowl, cover, and place in the 'fridge for at least 8 hours, preferably overnight.

Read the churning and freezing section on page 23, and freeze the ice cream in your churner according to the manufacturer's instructions. It typically takes between 20 – 30 minutes to freeze.

Once the ice cream has frozen to a soft-serve consistency in the churner, pour the cocoa nibs through the opening in the top of the churner and churn until mixed through.

Quickly transfer the ice cream from the churning bowl into your pre-chilled container, and place in the deep freezer for at least 8 hours, preferably overnight.

~~~~~~

Sneaky money-saving tip: If you're going to make any quantity of this most delicious and refreshing of ice creams, I'd start growing your own mint. I planted a $1.50 shoot in a large pot, and 6 weeks later had enough mint to open a mint farm. Fresh mint also makes delicious Mint Tea, which is a god-send if you don't like drinking plain water or green tea as much as I don't.

Riveting Root Beer

1 ½ cup / 12 fl oz. thick coconut milk

1 cup / 8 fl oz. almond milk, vanilla unsweetened

½ cup / 4 fl oz. heavy (double) cream

4 ½ oz. / 125g xylitol

1 tsp. sea salt

1 tsp. vanilla extract

6 tsp. root beer extract

1 TBSP vegetable glycerin

2 ½ oz. / 75g vanilla 100% whey protein powder

½ tsp. guar gum

Place all ingredients EXCEPT the whey protein powder and guar gum, in a blender and blend for 10 seconds.

Turn the blender to low speed, and while the blender is running, add the whey protein powder, then the guar gum, through the opening in the lid, and blend for 5 seconds. Do not over blend.

Pour the ice cream mix into a bowl, cover, and place in the 'fridge for at least 8 hours, preferably overnight.

Read the churning and freezing section on page 23, and freeze the ice cream in your churner according to the manufacturer's instructions. It typically takes between 20 – 30 minutes to freeze.

Once the ice cream has frozen to a soft-serve consistency, quickly transfer it from the churning bowl into your pre-chilled container, and place in the deep freezer for at least 8 hours, preferably overnight.

~~~~~~

Sneaky laundry-saving tip: If you have never worked with root beer extract, it is the stain-iest stuff I have ever encountered. I thoroughly recommend wearing your oldest, grubbiest t-shirt while you're in the throes of making Root Beer Ice Cream, or root beer anything for that matter. Plus, save a kitchen countertop today! Wipe up any spills immediately!

I'd never had root beer until I landed on this side of the pond, but I quickly grew to love me a lovely, frothy root beer float. Now that I am a sugar-free zone, I had stopped partaking. Until now. Go on, pour some fizzy water over this Root Beer Ice Cream and have yourself a Root Beer Float. I dare you!

RECIPES: MIX-INS

Blueberry Sauce

10 oz. / 280g fresh blueberries

1 ¾ oz. / 50g xylitol

1 TBSP water

1 TBSP lemon juice

¼ tsp. guar gum

2 tsp. kirsch (cherry liqueur)

Put the blueberries and xylitol in a small pan, stir well, and heat until the blueberries become juicy and start to breakdown.

Add the water and lemon juice and stir well.

Sprinkle the guar gum even over the surface of the sauce and mix rapidly to disperse the gum evenly throughout.

Continue to stir over the heat until the mixture has thickened.

Remove from the heat, add the kirsch and stir well.

Leave to cool before placing in an air-tight container in the 'fridge until use.

~~~~~~

The first time I ever ate a blueberry I was living in Canada, way up in the Rocky Mountains, 3 hours west of Banff. That was also the first time I ate nachos, bought soft-serve in a waxed carton to take home, saw a 15" pizza, and roasted marshmallows over a camp fire; not to mention it was the first time I gobbled up thick American pancakes, and ate bacon with maple syrup all over it. Who knew I would encounter so many culinary firsts up in the Great White North? Fun times!

I hold a lot of fondness for Canada. There were so many firsts – I waterskied, rode horses, drove a truck, went to a rodeo – The Calgary Stampede no less! – saw bears in the wild, went to the World's Fair in Vancouver, wore shorts for 3 months straight, and fell in love with a particularly rugged and handsome Oil Driller called Kevin. We met over a garbage can at the Expo, but that's a whole other story that it's probably best I don't get into.

I'm not one for eating blueberries straight – in the raw so to speak – but make a sauce and layer it with cheesecake ice cream? Or make a green smoothie and toss some in? How about Lemon Blueberry Scones? YES, please!

There's blueberries galore over at www.carriebrown.com and click on the recipes link.

Pear Sauce

1 lb / 450g cored pears (skins on!)

1 oz. / 30g xylitol

2 TBSP lemon juice

½ tsp. glycerin

½ tsp. guar gum

2 tsp. Grand Marnier (orange liqueur)

Chop the pears roughly and put in a small pan with the xylitol and lemon juice.

Stir well, and heat until the pears are very soft.

Puree the pears in a blender and then press the pear puree through a fine mesh sieve.

Return the puree to the pan and heat gently.

In a tiny dish, mix the glycerin and the guar gum into a paste.

Add the paste to the pear puree while whisking rapidly to disperse the gum evenly throughout.

Continue to stir over the heat until the mixture has thickened.

Remove from the heat, add the orange liqueur and stir well.

Leave to cool before placing in an air-tight container in the 'fridge until use.

~~~~~~

Making caramel sauce with no sugar is the single most frustrating and challenging recipe I've ever worked on. I've lost count of how many versions I've messed with, but I think it is something like 17. We're closer to being friends now, although it was touch and go for quite a while there.

Xylitol is definitely not sugar when it comes to heating it. It does not respond to the normal sugar tricks of the trade, and requires some careful handling and a bit of trickery pokery. I did manage to get a glorious Caramel Sauce made, but it is too tricky and too finicky to replicate perfectly, and I ain't giving you a recipe that might not work well for you. Nope. Can't do it.

So I thought about what I could make that would at least *look* like caramel sauce, while adding a touch of sweetness to your ice cream world.

Ladies and gentlemen, I give you Pear Sauce: golden, sweet, and delicious. Saucy awesomeness until I can finally wrestle the Caramel Sauce into submission.

I partly blame the Caramel Sauce for me missing summer this year. Or maybe more accurate would be to say that I missed *being out* in the summer this year. And then, even that is not strictly true. I just haven't really left the bounds of my delightful little yard (garden), edged as it is by wisteria and clematis, and decorated with roses, delphiniums, lush green grass, and huge pots overflowing with purple and yellow pansies. Not to mention the lively green herb garden growing nicely down one end – chives, sage, lemon thyme, and an ocean of mint. Yes, my yard has provided a most glorious spot to write a book. Writing this book for you was a most excellent reason not to leave my own little piece of land. Another excellent reason though, was pears.

Pears are important. Important enough to stay home and create recipes with. It is, after all, the season for pears – although it's tough to tell what is actually *in season* these days. Grocery stores far and wide have the requisite magical powers to conjure up every fruit known to man and parade them, scantily dressed, before us year-round. Notwithstanding our ability to have pears whenever we darn well please, which – strange creatures that we are – would usually reduce our desire to have them, pears are big on my things-to-love list.

I doubt you were expecting pears in ice cream, but I do try to keep things exciting for you. I know pears in ice cream isn't quite the adventure that a summer road trip to Wyoming or Montana might conjure up, but really, for fat-burning, health-boosting ice cream desperados searching for a way out, pears could be just the ticket.

It seems to me that pears have always been paired up with apples – like twins who were allowed to dress separately – with apples always assuming the role of first-born. Apples are everyone's favorite, pears their shy, retiring cousin. But I really have a penchant for pears, and I reasoned that having already injected pear deliciousness into smoothies, soups, porridge, salads, and vegetable sides, I must be able to use pear's considerable charms in ice cream.

Imagine my delight then, when I was able to ripple a full pound of pale green, smooth-skinned, drippingly juicy pears through vanilla ice cream studded with roasted hazelnuts. And if you could even imagine how much glee there was in my kitchen when I finally managed to coax fresh, ripe pears into a smooth and creamy ice cream dotted with crunchy poppy seeds. Worth another day or three in my own back yard, right there.

I poached pears on TV once, in orange liqueur, until they were spoon-soft and melt-in-your-mouth scrumptious. Then I poured warm chocolate sauce all over them and called it dessert. Back in those days I was still entertaining sugar, and had no problem with that sugary sauce slipping all over. While those heady sugar-filled days are over, I couldn't leave you stranded now that you want warm, sweet, juicy pears swathed in orange liqueur and swimming in chocolate. So you can just go ahead and use the next recipe in all its sugar-free gloriousness – Chocolate Fudge Ripple – to pour over your pears.

See what I did there? I love it when a plan comes together.

Want more pears? www.carriebrown.com and click on the recipes link, then search for pears.

Chocolate Fudge Ripple

1 cup / 8 fl oz. thick coconut milk

5 oz. / 140g sugar-free marshmallows (recipe page 105)

1 oz. / 30g cocoa powder, unsweetened

4 oz. / 110g 100% cocoa solids chocolate (unsweetened), chopped

¼ cup / 2 fl oz. vegetable glycerin

½ tsp. vanilla extract

Warn the thick coconut milk in a pan over medium heat.

Add the sugar-free marshmallows to the pan and stir constantly until the marshmallows are completely melted.

Sieve the cocoa powder directly into the pan, and whisk well until completely mixed into the marshmallow mixture.

Remove the pan from the heat and add the chopped chocolate. Stir well until the chocolate is completely melted.

Add the glycerin and vanilla extract and stir well.

Pour into a glass bowl or dish and leave to cool completely.

Once cold, cover and store in a cool, dark place - like a pantry or kitchen cupboard.

~~~~~~

This ripple is extremely thick. And dark, and shiny, and chocolaty, and utterly, utterly glorious. It's also quick and easy to sling together once you've got the sugar-free marshmallows made. It is extremely stable and does not freeze any harder than it is when it is completely cooled.

When I created this final version and realized it had worked, I was so happy I cried. And then I danced around the Marmalade HQ kitchen like a loon. If only you knew the trials and tribulations that I've been through to get you a fantastic sugar-free Chocolate Fudge Ripple for your ice cream. One that stays soft, and gooey, and luscious at -18C.

You're so worth it.

PS. If you make it a while in advance and it goes dull or stiffens, just warm gently and let cool again.

Lemon Curd

4 eggs

7 oz. / 200g xylitol

⅓ cup / 2 ½ fl oz. lemon juice (approx. 2 lemons)

Zest of 1 lemon

4 oz. / 110g coconut oil, melted

4 oz. / 110g butter, melted

Whisk the eggs well with a fork and pour into a small pan.

Add the xylitol, lemon juice, lemon zest, coconut oil, and butter.

Whisk ingredients together well.

Place on the stove over a medium heat and STIR CONSTANTLY as the mixture slowly thickens. It takes 12 – 15 minutes to thicken fully. Embrace it. Be patient.

DO NOT ALLOW THE MIXTURE TO BOIL – it will curdle, or you will get scrambled eggs.

When the mixture is thick enough to coat the back of a spoon, quickly remove it from the heat and pour it through a fine mesh sieve into a glass, lidded container (such as a Pyrex storage bowl). No, you cannot omit this step. It must be sieved!

Stir the mixture in the sieve until you are left with only the zest pulp and a few strands of egg. Use a second, clean spatula to scrape the underside of the sieve as you go.

Once all the curd has been passed through the sieve, leave uncovered until completely cold, stirring every 10 minutes to prevent a skin from forming.

When cold, put the lid on the container and place in the 'fridge. Once chilled it will be thick and spreadable.

~~~~~~

Afraid of making egg custards? Don't be! I used to be, but I've discovered that egg custards are easy, beautiful, and making them is downright therapeutic. Egg custards taught me that the fear is always worse than the reality. Me and egg custards are best buds now, and they are the finest excuse I know to stand by the stove and do nothing except gaze lovingly into a saucepan and stir the contents. These days, when I need a break from doing, I make something that requires an egg custard; just so I can stand still for 12 minutes. Egg custards rock.

In other news, not only are egg custards awesome to make, but this Lemon Curd makes my mouth insanely happy. Tart, sweet, silky smooth. GO, lemons!

Lemon Shortbread Cookies

7 oz. / 200g almond flour (ground almonds)

1 oz. / 30g finely ground chia seeds (white chia looks prettier, but black works fine)

2½ oz. / 70g xylitol

1 tsp. xanthan gum

Zest of 2 lemons

3 oz. / 85g cold butter

Put the almond flour, ground chia seeds, xylitol, xanthan gum, and lemon zest in a food processor and pulse a couple of times to mix well.

Cut the butter into small squares and add to the dry ingredients in the processor.

Pulse until it resembles fine breadcrumbs.

Pulse a couple more times and it will start to ball together.

Turn out onto a work surface and lightly knead to form a soft dough.

Roll into a sausage shape about 1.5" in diameter.

Use a serrated edge knife to slice the dough sausage into slices.

Place the slices on a baking sheet sprayed with coconut oil, and bake in the center of the oven at 300F, for 20 – 23 minutes until they are golden brown.

Remove from the oven and leave to cool on the baking sheet. Step away from the cookies!

Once cool, move the cookies to a cooking rack and leave until completely cold.

Pack in an airtight container and leave overnight if you can possibly manage it, before you eat them. I know, I know. Trust me, they are better if left.

~~~~~~

It's the truth, the whole truth, and nothing but the truth: I. LOVE. LEMON. Anything lemon. The more lemony the better, really. Lemon has the ability to transform something quite ordinary with just the swift swipe of a microplane. Like these Lemon Shortbread Cookies. One minute they're regular little shortbread cookies, and the next they're alive and zesty – bits of yellow peel baked right in – giving miniature bursts of luscious lemon to every crumbly bite.

Bonus! These babies are gluten-free, grain-free, sugar-free and can be thrown together in a New York minute. What's not to love?

Peanut Butter Drops

1 cup / 8 fl oz. smooth peanut butter, unsweetened

1 TBSP glycerin

1 oz coconut flour

4 tsp. konjac flour / glucomannan powder

Leave the jar of peanut butter at room temperature overnight so that it softens.

Put the peanut butter in a bowl with the glycerin and mix well.

Sieve the coconut flour and konjac flour together into a separate bowl and mix well.

Add the mixed flours into the peanut butter in 4 batches, mixing well after each addition.

When all the flours are well incorporated, cover and place in the 'fridge until the peanut butter stiffens.

Line a flat plate with plastic wrap, and pull small pieces of peanut butter out of the bowl and place on the plate. Once all the peanut butter has been divided into little pieces, place the peanut butter drops in the freezer on the plate.

Once frozen, if you are storing the peanut butter balls for any length of time before adding them to your ice cream, remove from the plate and place in a glass, airtight container, using greaseproof paper between the layers.

~~~~~~

Sneaky peanut butter tip: if you buy peanut butter freshly made from a store that has a peanut butter grinder, you may need to add more coconut and konjac flours to this recipe as this kind of peanut butter tends to be softer than peanut butter in a jar. I used Trader Joe's Smooth Peanut Butter in this recipe. Make sure to check the label if you buy pre-packaged peanut butter. The only ingredients should be peanuts and salt.

Sugar-free Marshmallows

¼ cup / 2 fl oz. cold water

1 TBSP powdered gelatin

5 ¼ oz. / 150g xylitol

¼ cup / 2 fl oz. hot water

¼ cup / 2 fl oz. vegetable glycerin

1 tsp. vanilla extract

Powdered xylitol

Spray a cookie tray with coconut oil spray and set aside.

Put the cold water in a small dish and sprinkle the powdered gelatin slowly and evenly over the surface so that it dissolves in the water. Set aside.

Place the xylitol, hot water, and vegetable glycerin in a small pan over a high heat.

The xylitol will melt and become clear.

Gently add the softened gelatin to the pan and stir carefully until it has dissolved.

Once the gelatin has dissolved, allow the syrup to come to the boil.

CAUTION! MELTED XYLITOL IS RIDICULOUSLY HOT. Don't be scared, but PLEASE BE CAREFUL. (The boiling point of water is 100 °C. The boiling point of xylitol is 212 °C. That's hot.)

Carefully, and slowly to avoid splashes, pour the boiling syrup into a large glass mixing bowl, or the bowl of your stand mixer, if you have one.

Add the vanilla extract, and then whisk on HIGH – either in your stand mixer or with a hand mixer – for 15 minutes. Yes, 15 minutes. If you use a hand mixer you will start to hate me at about the 4 ½ minute mark because it will feel like 15 minutes already and you still have 10 ½ to go.

As you whisk, the syrup will transform into a white, fluffy meringue-like mass. After 15 minutes you will get stiff peaks, like meringue.

Transfer the marshmallow into a piping bag with a small plain nozzle in it. Pipe small blobs of marshmallow onto the cookie trays sprayed with coconut oil.

Lightly sieve powdered xylitol over the marshmallows, and leave to set for several hours. Store in an airtight glass container using greaseproof or waxed paper between the layers.

Note: This recipes makes enough for one batch of mix-ins and one batch of Chocolate Fudge Ripple.

Sugar-free Meringue Cookies

3 fresh egg whites (pasteurized whites will not whip)

½ TBSP lemon juice

5 oz. / 140 g xylitol

Pre-heat oven to 225F.

Place the egg whites in a large mixing bowl, add the lemon juice and whisk using either a stand- or hand-mixer until the egg whites have formed stiff, dry peaks.

Add the xylitol, a tablespoon at a time, whisking very well between each addition.

Once you have added the last of the xylitol, continue whisking until the meringue is stiff and very glossy.

Using a piping bag with the nozzle of your choice, fill the bag with meringue and pipe small shapes onto a baking tray lined with parchment paper.

Place the baking sheet(s) in the center of the pre-heated oven and bake for 2 hours.

After 2 hours, turn the oven off and leave the meringues in the warm oven overnight.

If the meringues are still sticky in the morning, leave them in the oven until they are dry, or if you need the oven, place them somewhere dry until they are ready. This could take up to 2 days. Patience is a virtue.

~~~~~~

Sneaky go-faster tip: if you don't have the time – or the inclination – for all that waiting, but you really, really want to make Lemon Meringue Pie Ice Cream, use sugar-free marshmallows instead (recipe on page 105). You will have soft white bits instead of crunchy white bits, but the taste will be very similar.

If you want more sugar-less meringue-making tips: head over to www.carriebrown.com, click on the recipes link, and type 'Meringue Cookies' in the search box.

~~~~~~

To me, this recipe is the ultimate giving-the-finger to sugar. Oh my. Did I really just type that out loud? But really, it's true. What is meringue except a bit of egg white holding a whole ton of sugar in suspension? Well now you can have your meringues, and eat them too. I must admit, it still feels incredibly naughty eating sugar-less meringues, even though it isn't. Take THAT, sugar!

WHERE TO GET MORE COOL STUFF

CarrieBrown.com

Recipes! Recipes! Recipes! Fat-burning, health-boosting, delicious goodness, with tips and tricks for living a healthy lifestyle.

BailorGroup.com

Free support group, free 28 day eating and exercise program, and free daily tips.

SmarterScienceOfSlim.com

Health and fitness Podcast & Blog.

CalorieMythBook.com

Exclusive previews and bonus content for the revolutionary health book.

www.carriebrown.com

The "kids" eating their greens.

Clockwise from top left:

Daisy, Chiko (RIP), Dougal, Penelope, and Zebedee.

Florence is MIA, but I expect she is either staring at the dishwasher or wondering what just happened.

110

I realize all decent authors write this bit in the third person, but I am not convinced I qualify for the "decent" category, so I am just going to write this like the rest of the book: real, rambunctious, and slightly irreverent. I like life better that way.

I am a British American ex-professional pastry chef with a crazy, 4-country, 3-continent-spanning resume which includes such things as a chocolate TV show, a chocolate cookbook & making pastries for the Queen of England. I trained at the National Bakery School in London.

These days I use my pastry chef talents to create scrumptious recipes to help the world eat smarter, live better, and put the 'healthy' back into healthy again.

I am Podcast Co-host, Recipe Developer, and Food Photographer for the Smarter Science of Slim, working excitedly and tirelessly alongside Jonathan Bailor.

The only other note-worthy attributes are my humongous appetite, an accent like crack (apparently), and a love for people who keep on going when the going gets tough. I also think leeks are the finest vegetables on earth.

I live in Seattle with a couple of large cameras, a ridiculous amount of cocoa powder, and a pile of cats – Florence, Dougal, Penelope, Zebedee, Daisy, and Mr. McHenry. We love it here.

Printed in Great Britain
by Amazon.co.uk, Ltd.,
Marston Gate.